Steven Soderbergh |

Contemporary Film Directors

Edited by James Naremore

The Contemporary Film Directors series provides concise, well-written introductions to directors from around the world and from every level of the film industry. Its chief aims are to broaden our awareness of important artists, to give serious critical attention to their work, and to illustrate the variety and vitality of contemporary cinema. Contributors to the series include an array of internationally respected critics and academics. Each volume contains an incisive critical commentary, an informative interview with the director, and a detailed filmography.

A list of books in the series appears at the end of this book.

Steven Soderbergh |

Aaron Baker

UNIVERSITY
OF
ILLINOIS
PRESS
URBANA
CHICAGO
SPRINGFIELD

Manufactured in the United States of America
1 2 3 4 5 C P 5 4 3 2 1
<IC> This book is printed on acid-free paper.

Library of Congress Cataloging-in-Publication Data
Baker, Aaron.
Steven Soderbergh / Aaron Baker.
p. cm.
Includes bibliographical references and index.
Includes filmography.
ISBN-13: 978-0-252-03605-7 (hardcover: alk. paper)
ISBN-10: 0-252-03605-0 (hardcover: alk. paper)
ISBN-13: 978-0-252-07796-8 (pbk.:alk. paper)
ISBN-10: 0-252-07796-2 (pbk.: alk. paper)
1. Soderbergh, Steven, 1963—Criticism and interpretation.
I. Title.
PN1998.3.S593B35   2011
791.4302'33092—dc22   2010045988

Contents |

Preface and Acknowledgments |

Studies of film authorship often focus on the explication of a director's worldview and formal choices as the basis for a broader analysis of social issues and larger stylistic tendencies. The following commentary employs that pattern. I argue that Steven Soderbergh practices an eclectic type of moviemaking that is indebted both to the European art cinema and the Hollywood genre film. His films diverge from the contemporary Hollywood mainstream through the statements they offer on issues— including political repression, illegal drugs, violence, environmental degradation, the empowering and controlling potential of digital technology, and economic injustice—using a combination of realism and expressive stylization of character subjectivity. Soderbergh has imported these thematic and formal variations into Hollywood genre films featuring A-list stars, bringing an independent aesthetic to large audiences. Although Soderbergh to date has made twenty feature films, I focus on four movies—*Out of Sight* (1998), *The Limey* (1999), *Traffic* (2000), and *Ocean's Eleven* (2001)—because they best illustrate his dominant formal and thematic patterns but also the hybrid flexibility that has made his career so influential.

Soderbergh has most recently released three films: *Che* (2008), about the Argentine revolutionary Che Guevara; *The Girlfriend Experience* (2009), a case study of an expensive escort played by the adult-film star Sasha Grey; and *The Informant!* (2009), an exposé of corporate crime. The *Variety* reviewer Todd McCarthy calls *Che* "a commercial impossibility," its narrative "a jigsaw puzzle," and the battle scenes "clinical." He criticizes the film for depicting "American and Latin American authorities . . . as cardboard mouthpieces of imperialism and abusive dictatorships" and bemoans that Benicio Del Toro as Che "is not allowed to be much of an action hero" and at times "becomes a secondary character." A. O. Scott, writing in the *New York Times* about *The Girlfriend Experience*, praises its effective use of high-definition video cinematography and a nonprofessional cast to tell a story "less interested in sex than in money, which is shown to be a far more powerful and dangerous source of obsession, confusion, passion, and calculation." Yet Scott qualifies such praise by writing that, due to Grey's lack of acting skills, the story's fractured chronology, and the movie's "chilly, observant style," *The Girlfriend Experience* cannot generate much "dramatic life." These critical reviews reflect the commercial expectations now associated with Soderbergh's films but also the traits that have often put them at odds with most of what Hollywood produces: nonlinear narratives, an aura of realism, a willingness to take critical political positions, and a subordination of star personae to characters.

The Informant! again demonstrates Soderbergh's ability to work within the American commercial film industry even while subverting some of its main assumptions. With Matt Damon—whose seventy-seven-million-dollar average earnings per film is the highest of any of the stars Soderbergh has collaborated with—saturation marketing, and a return to the social-protest film based on a true story, which he had done so successfully with *Erin Brockovich* (2000), *The Informant!* demonstrates Soderbergh's tendency to adopt the commercial strategies of stars and genre, yet without reinforcing Hollywood's ideology of happy endings based on the strength of individual protagonists. Damon's role as Marc Whitacre, an Archer Daniels Midland vice president who blows the whistle on price fixing, but who also turns out to have been embezzling nine million dollars from the company, underscores the thematic continuity of Soderbergh's last three films by keeping the focus on class inequality and the moral choice of rejecting or complying with an ethos of extreme self-interest. The film's style initially seems noncommittal. Michael Atkinson calls it "deliberately affectless . . . rarely going for laughs or drama but instead maintaining a mask of uninflected objectivity throughout, as if *it* were covering up a web of lies as well." But by showing how Whitacre's duplicitous self-interest results in his getting more time in prison than the bigwigs he fingers, and emphasizing how that unfair outcome results from the decisions that Damon's character makes, Soderbergh suggests the limitations of the assumption that

Hollywood films are "better" than those made in the rest of the world because they "sell something that people *want* . . . the Unstated State Religion of America: Individualism" (Suber). Soderbergh's cautionary statement in *The Informant!* fits with his brand of hybrid filmmaking, which allows him to work within the industry but also to avoid what Atkinson calls its "mainstream manipulativeness."

Damon's presence in *The Informant!* also demonstrates how the challenge and innovation of films such as *Traffic, Solaris* (2002), *Full Frontal* (2002), *The Good German* (2006), and *Che* have helped Soderbergh attract stars. He has worked with George Clooney, Brad Pitt, Catherine Zeta-Jones, Julia Roberts, Cate Blanchett, Benicio Del Toro, and Michael Douglas because of their interest in not only latching onto a director who has had box-office success but in collaboration with Soderbergh's risk-taking and expansion of their creative skills. As a result, even Soderbergh's popular, star-driven genre films like *Ocean's Eleven* or *Traffic* are smarter, less violent, and more socially engaged than most. When asked by an interviewer if he traded commercial projects for the opportunity to do personal films, Soderbergh responded: "No, they're all [personal] for me, even the *Ocean's* movies. I don't spend two years of my life on stuff that I'm not into" (Epstein).

While John Caldwell concedes the importance of Andrew Sarris's idea of film authorship as the director "maintaining artistic control of all elements of the filmmaking process without studio intervention," he also asserts that "negotiated and collective authorship is an almost unavoidable and determining reality in contemporary film/television" (198–99). Soderbergh is quick to give credit to his collaborators, whether they be actors like Roberts, Clooney, and Del Toro, the writer Scott Frank, the composers Cliff Martinez and David Holmes, or the production designer Philip Messina. His tendency to allude to other movies and acknowledge openly his use of ideas from these films is another way he underlines the collaborative nature of his work.

Soderbergh's appeal to star actors comes from his collaborative generosity, the opportunities he gives them for creative growth, but also from his use of a guerilla style of shooting with handheld cameras, small crews, and single lighting setups. His willingness to work fast and cheap in this manner, because it contributes to his reputation for being "frugal, a workaholic," and a filmmaker who makes movies that "stars

[are] anxious to be in," has allowed Soderbergh to follow his creative inclinations and experiment (Taubin, "Degraded Dupes"). This stripped-down, fast-paced method of shooting also promotes the realism that he favors, supports actors' performances by keeping them in character, and preserves his authorial control, as he has been the principal camera operator and editor for these projects (Caldwell 229–30).

Moreover, Soderbergh's approach on another recent film, *The Good German*, shows just how skillfully he manages to retain creative control. Knowing he was taking a risk by making a thirty-two-million-dollar black-and-white film with no hero or happy ending, Soderbergh returned to the classic-era style of shooting with carefully lit setups, fixed focal-length lenses, boom mics, and less coverage. He therefore made a film that could only be assembled one way: "It was shot to go together very, very specifically," he commented (Kehr 15).

Soderbergh's ability to work in both of these modes—in a guerilla style as well as on a classic-era soundstage—shows him to be a film-maker whose conception of authorship is as hybridized as the movies he makes: in some ways compromising with the commercial demands of Hollywood, and in others fiercely independent in defending his creative principles.

Likewise, my own production process has been a combination of collaboration and blind faith. I want to thank Peter Lehman and Daniel Bernardi for listening to my ideas about Soderbergh and giving me the time and support to write about his films. I am also very grateful to Jim Naremore and Joan Catapano, who have shown tremendous patience and confidence in my work. Most of all I wish to express my gratitude to Maria Martell for encouragement and exposure to new perspectives that have helped me grow in so many ways.

Steven Soderbergh |

The Films of Steven Soderbergh |

Relational Independence

Steven Soderbergh's twenty feature films present a diverse range of subject matter and formal styles. They range from his 1989 breakthrough hit *Sex, Lies, and Videotape*, about the sex lives of four twentysomethings, to social-problem films such as *King of the Hill* (1993), *Erin Brockovich* (2000), *Traffic* (2000), *Che* (2008), and *The Informant!* (2009). Carefully stylized noir in *Kafka* (1991), *The Underneath* (1995), and *The Good German* (2006) contrasts with the digital-video improvisation of *Full Frontal* (2002), *Bubble* (2006), and *The Girlfriend Experience* (2009). In *Gray's Anatomy* (1996), Spalding Gray does performance art, while *Out of Sight* (1998), *The Limey* (1999), and *Solaris* (2002) are genre films deconstructed by an element of modernist discontinuity. Even the cost of making his films has shown great variety, ranging from the six-figure budget for *Schizopolis* (1996) to the star-studded *Ocean's* series blockbusters (2001, 2004, 2007) that averaged nearly one hundred million dollars to produce.

The eclecticism in Soderbergh's movies would appear to invalidate a claim to the distinctive style typical of film authorship. Moreover, one might point to his more commercial projects as evidence of a lack of creative integrity in his work. However, I would argue for the importance of Soderbergh's films for reasons that don't entirely discount these critiques but rather show how the variety of his work and the commercial viability of some of his films are prominent aspects of his individual style. Soderbergh's movies merit a closer look because of his insistence on what David Bordwell calls "art-cinema narration," characterized by complexity and respect for the audience that have too often been lacking in the American cinema during Soderbergh's career as a director ("Authorship" 42). Yet another reason for my interest in Soderbergh's work has to do precisely with his movies that have made large amounts of money, in particular *Erin Brockovich, Traffic, Ocean's Eleven,* and *Ocean's Thirteen.* Rather than simply part of a strategy of making commercial projects to finance more personal films, these movies employ the utopian resolve of Hollywood narrative—an optimistic determination to overcome injustice or inequality—yet contextualize it by representing some of the social determinants of these problems in a way that resonates with large audiences without capitulating to a condescending blockbuster recipe of high-concept, digitally enhanced violence and commodified synergy. Even Soderbergh's most commercial movies offer some of the complexity and critical challenges to viewers found in his art films.

An additional characteristic of the films that Soderbergh has directed that supports an assertion of authorial control is his hands-on involvement in various aspects of their production: he has written five of his features, edited seven, and done the cinematography for eleven, including everything since *Traffic.* Soderbergh's contribution to these important aspects of the filmmaking process has resulted in a large degree of thematic and formal continuity across his apparently diverse range of movies. He consistently builds stories around characters alienated from a world that values wealth, power, and self-interest, and resolution of the conflicts involving such outsider protagonists rarely takes the form of the neat, individualized responses typical of Hollywood. Although he adopts his style to fit the topic at hand, and it therefore varies as much as his subjects, the form in Soderbergh's films often breaks through the fourth wall to create discontinuity that communicates the unconventional thinking of such marginalized characters, sets up critical distance for the viewer, or uses self-reflexivity, allusion, or realism to comment on a particular narrative situation.

Born in Baton Rouge, Louisiana, in 1963, Soderbergh has stated in interviews that he watched a lot of films growing up and that his university-professor father, Peter Soderbergh, "would let me see anything" (Kaufman 30). Steven showed a talent for drawing, and at age fourteen, his dad enrolled him in an animation class at Louisiana State University. The younger Soderbergh soon began shooting live-action films and continued making movies through high school. At seventeen, he bypassed college and moved to Los Angeles, where he worked for several years as a screenwriter and editor. An editing job on a music video for the British rock group Yes led to an offer to make a documentary for the band, *9021Live* (1986), that was nominated for a Grammy award. Soderbergh wrote the initial draft of the script for his first feature, *Sex, Lies, and Videotape,* during a weeklong cross-country trip in 1988 and shot it the following year, primarily with money that RCA/Columbia Home Video had paid in advance for the film's video rights.

Although *Sex, Lies, and Videotape* took its audience appeal to a new level, by the time it was released in 1989 American independent cinema was already firmly in place. Filmmakers such as John Sayles, Jim Jarmusch, the Coen brothers, Spike Lee, and David Lynch had all found audiences for their movies in the 1980s, aided by the rapid growth in home video but also because they offered an alternative to the dominant tendencies in Hollywood movies. Contrary to the pattern in American movie history—from the founding of United Artists in 1919, through the B pictures of Republic and Monogram, to package production since the 1950s—of films made outside the studio system that were not very different from most of what came from the studio system, the independent cinema of the 1980s was distinguished by its stylistic variation that "disrupts the continuity of Hollywood formal style" or in its "challenging perspectives on social issues" (King, *American Independent,* 2). Peter Biskind sums up the appeal of independent films from this period by emphasizing their strong positions on "controversial" issues and a kind of artisanal quality: "If Hollywood sold fantasy and escapism, indies thrived on realism and engagement. If Hollywood avoided controversial subjects, indies embraced them. If Hollywood movies were expensive, indie films were cheap. . . . Hollywood favored spectacle, action, and special effects, while indies worked on a more intimate scale, privileging script and emphasizing character and mise-en-scène" (19). Michael Z. Newman has emphasized the lower cost of independent films as indicative of a creative freedom that came to be equated with aesthetic quality: "[A] low budget would itself become a discursive fetish object, a means of concretizing a nebulous quality (honesty, truth, vision)" (19).

While distinctly different from most Hollywood films in their foregrounding of social engagement, realism, or what Geoff King calls "more complex, stylized, expressive . . . forms," the independent films of the 1980s were still mostly narrative (10). Some of these movies therefore generated good earnings in relation to their modest production budgets: Jarmusch made *Stranger Than Paradise* (1984) for just ninety thousand dollars, and it earned almost $2.5 million. Sayles's *Brother from Another Planet* (1986), produced for four hundred thousand dollars, made $3.7 million. And Spike Lee spent just $175,000 on his feature debut *She's Gotta Have It* (1986), which took in seven million dollars.

Despite such good earnings, none of the 1980s independents had gone beyond twenty-five million in revenue until *Sex, Lies, and Videotape* demonstrated the possibility of a larger audience, primarily because the co-chairmen at Miramax Films, Harvey and Bob Weinstein, made the bold move of spending $2.5 million on prints and advertising, more than double the production budget, and put it on more screens than was the norm for an independent film. Conventional thinking in 1989 dictated that you don't exhibit art or independent films in mall multiplexes or place more than a four-inch advertisement in the newspaper on opening day. Miramax, however, spent heavily on television ads for *Sex, Lies, and Videotape* and opened it on six hundred screens, including suburban mall theaters, like just another Hollywood movie. This investment in wider marketing and distribution, combined with a rave review from Todd McCarthy in *Variety* and the buzz created from the awards it won at Sundance and Cannes, took *Sex, Lies, and Videotape* to unprecedented earnings for an independent film, more than fifty million dollars worldwide (Biskind 82). As an exception to his observation that frugality and exclusivity became primary values of American independent cinema, Newman describes Soderbergh as "admired for retaining an indie sensibility even when making movies with wider appeal" (20). The Weinstein brothers would go on to drive the crossover success of independent film in the 1990s—most notably with *Pulp Fiction* (1994)—by playing on this belief that an alternative vision could coexist with expensive advertising, wide distribution, and star actors.

Sex, Lies, and Videotape displayed the skillful balance of commercial and personal cinema found in Soderbergh's later films such as *Out of Sight, Erin Brockovich, Traffic, Ocean's Eleven,* and *Ocean's Thirteen.* With only five thousand dollars in his budget for set design, Soderbergh shot his debut film entirely on location in Baton Rouge, using long takes and slow tracking shots to preserve the temporal and spatial integrity of the narrative world and overlapping dialogue—that he claimed he borrowed from *The Graduate* (1967)—to further support a realist style (DVD commentary). Moreover, Soderbergh has acknowledged a personal investment in the story about the sexual entanglements of John (Peter Gallagher), a yuppie lawyer who typifies the self-interest associated with the 1980s; his wife, Ann (Andie McDowell); her sister, Cynthia (Laura San Giacomo); and John's college roommate, Graham (James Spader). After learning of his affair with Cynthia, Ann leaves John for Graham, resulting in an upbeat conclusion that Soderbergh defended for its truthfulness: "I changed the ending in a more positive direction

Figure 1. Long take and tracking shot in
Sex, Lies, and Videotape.

. . . not out of compromise. My personal experience has taught me that after periods of torment . . . you learn that the hardships you have had taught you something" (Kaufman 21).

The ending of *Sex, Lies, and Videotape* also makes a broader statement about the importance of connection and responsibility to others, a theme that runs through many of Soderbergh's films. The previously distant Graham finds he needs Ann; the title character in *Kafka* (Jeremy Irons) leaves his creative isolation to engage in political subversion, and at the end of the film he writes to his parents, "I now can no longer deny that I am part of the world around me." In *King of the Hill*, the young protagonist, Aaron (Jesse Bradford), and his family are saved by the father's WPA job. *Traffic* shows the Michael Douglas character sacrificing his career ambitions to help his addicted daughter and reunite his family; likewise, the cop characters in that film (Benecio Del Toro, Don Cheadle, Luis Guzman) act to protect their disadvantaged communities. In *Erin Brockovich*, the title character (Julia Roberts) finds meaning working in a class-action suit that provides justice for hundreds of people victimized by a utility company. In *Solaris*, George Clooney's character leaves behind life on earth to try again with his wife in outer space. Despite their star power and veneer of glamor, the *Ocean's* movies are also about the importance of teamwork and loyalty, and as much revenue as these big-budget films generated, they ultimately endorse those two values over money. *The Underneath, Out of Sight, The Limey, Bubble*, and *The Good German* present negative examples, returning tragic results for characters who can't connect with other people. Finally, *Che*, the story of a man who martyred himself on behalf of communist revolution in the developing world, takes the idea of responsibility to others about as far as it can go.

Sex, Lies, and Videotape won the Audience Prize at Sundance and the Palme d'Or in Cannes, beating out Spike Lee's *Do the Right Thing* at the French festival because, according to the jury chair Wim Wenders, the latter film lacked a heroic character (Taubin, "Fear"). Justin Wyatt sees the appeal of the Graham character less as heroic than for his autoeroticism aided by videotape as a practical response to the late-1980s concern about safe sex in the era of AIDS (79). Geoff King describes the film's alternative sexuality as offering a selling point for American independents; Graham exemplifies how characters "defined as sexually deviant by mainstream society turn up disproportionately often in indie films," creating a *"frisson* that can be marketable" (*American Independent* 200).

The strong earnings for *Sex, Lies, and Videotape,* along with the rapid growth of video and cable markets, fueled the increase in the number of American independent films released in the early 1990s (Maltby 219). Yet, such revenue success was a mixed blessing, as it drove up expectations for earnings, setting what Soderbergh called "an unrealistic benchmark for other [independent] films" (Wyatt 80). As production and marketing costs rose, and without the theatrical release and appeal to the family market needed to spur video rentals and sales, many smaller films generated little profit (Maltby 219). The success of independent cinema spurred production to the point of oversupply. By the end of the 1990s, according to King, thirteen to fifteen hundred features were being made each year, many of which wouldn't find a distributor (*American Independent* 36). To compound the problem for independent filmmakers, higher profit expectations encouraged videos stores to emphasize depth rather than range of copy, so that shelves contained mostly well-publicized films. Sell-through strategies aimed at getting consumers to buy films for home viewing also favored movies with larger marketing budgets (24). As the major media corporations entered the independent market, beginning in 1993 with Disney's purchase of Miramax and Time Warner's acquisition of New Line three years later, money was increasingly shifted to fewer, safer projects during production rather than more adventurous films after they were made (45).

Soderbergh's next three movies following *Sex, Lies, and Videotape* did get distributed to theaters but also resisted the market reality he had helped create by resembling European art cinema with alienated protagonists, stylized form, and ambiguous endings. His second film, *Kafka,* presents neither a straightforward biography of the Czech writer nor an adaptation of his fiction but instead a representation of experiences that Kafka would later put into his novels, reflecting what Soderbergh called "the manipulation of the individual by the State and the more or less unconscious complicity with evil" (Kaufman 51). Soderbergh shot *Kafka* in black and white and asked Jeremy Irons to play the title character passively for most of the film, reacting with diffidence to a shadowy expressionist world of political oppression. Even when Kafka rebels by planting a bomb inside the Castle, Prague's citadel of government control, this action's resemblance to earlier ineffective attacks by a small group of anarchists implies the futility of such violent resistance. Moreover, the title character may have decided to act, but near the end of the film he also accepts the statement of a police inspector (Armin Muller Stahl) that a fellow insurgent committed suicide—when in fact she had been tortured—and we last see Kafka in an image of confinement, framed by the window of his room.

Soderbergh's portrayal of Kafka as alienated but lacking a viable alternative ideology fits with Bill Dodd's statement that the writer "was certainly familiar with, and appears to have been sympathetic to, radical political theory of the left, but neither his biography nor his fiction suggests that he subscribed to a conventional political philosophy or programme" (146). While Dodd concludes that the notion that Kafka was "in any sense a political writer . . . is still somewhat contentious in Kafka scholarship" (131), Iris Bruce has traced the more accepted idea that Kafka's Jewish identity was an influence on his fiction (150). As an example of this influence, Bruce notes that the transformation that affects Gregor Samsa in Kafka's *Metamorphosis* (1912) "in Jewish forklore [is] generally inflicted as a punishment for transgression" (151). Kafka lived during a period of widespread anti-Semitism—in 1897, when he was fourteen, there were three days of anti-Jewish riots in his home city of Prague—Sander Gilman argues that the writer chose to counter negative stereotypes of Jews as "pathological" and intellectuals as "feminized and marginalized" by "recontextualizing these painful discourses in an ostensibly non Jewish 'universal' discourse, namely . . . modernism" (qtd. in Dodd 143). Therefore, echoes of the notorious Dreyfus Affair, in which a Jewish army officer was exiled from France for treason, appear—but without specific reference to Judaism—in *The Metamorphosis* and *The Trial* (1925). Similarily, Soderbergh evades anti-Semitic and anti-intellectual stereotypes by employing the conventions of American cinema to deemphasize ethnicity and to rely on male protagonists who take matters into their own hands: he doesn't identify the anarchists—Kafka included—as Jewish, and the title character defies stereotypes of intellectuals as weak and irrelevant by acting violently against the oppressive state.

While the emotional reawakening at the end of *Sex, Lies, and Videotape* probably contributed to its audience appeal, Soderbergh's third film, *King of the Hill*, like *Kafka*, leaves its conflict between agency and alienation unresolved. Based on E. H. Hotchner's memoir of his childhood in Depression-era St. Louis, *King of the Hill* presents an unflinching depiction of the deprivations that twelve-year-old Aaron experiences but also bathes the story in soft light and earth tones that evoke Hotchner's nostalgic remembrance of the period bolstered by faith in the New Deal. The hardships as well as the more optimistic perspectives come through the narrative's use of Aaron's vantage point: the boy's lack of awareness of the power of larger economic forces brought to bear on his life supports the story's optimism. He is a bright, creative, and likeable kid who finds some way to get through the challenges he faces. The film's conclusion also preserves Hoetcher's belief in the New Deal, saving Aaron's family from destitution when his father gets a WPA job. While government is the villain in *Kafka*, it becomes the savior in *King of the Hill*.

Along with Hotchner's positive outlook, however, *King of the Hill* also includes graphic representation of the brutal effects of the Depression. With his younger brother shipped off to relatives, his mother in a sanitarium with tuberculosis, and his father on the road selling watches, Aaron is left alone, reduced to eating magazine pictures of food that he must imagine are real. He sees his former neighbor, Mr. Sandoz (John Durbin), violently evicted from his room and later, pale and dazed from hunger, in a Hooverville. Another neighbor, Mr. Mungo (Spalding Gray), a poised and witty man who cites classical literature, slits his wrists and dies slumped over his sink after the neighborhood restaurant cuts off his credit. Earlier in the film, the boy is puzzled by a prostitute named Lydia (Elizabeth McGovern) in Mungo's room, but her presence fits with the other difficult conditions Aaron witnesses or faces himself without fully understanding them. Despite the warm colors and high-key lighting that imply Aaron's strength and perseverance, and the happy ending created by the father's job, the disturbing realities in *King of the Hill* limited its appeal to family audiences. Made on a budget of eight million dollars, it grossed just over one million and has not yet been released on DVD.

Soderbergh's fourth film, *The Underneath*, continues the focus on alienated protagonists while following the pattern in his first three films of alluding to other movies. Noel Carroll describes such allusionism as when "a new film . . . evokes . . . an old film" not only by reference to the first movie's fictional world but also through invocation of "a web of interrelated ideas previously introduced by film criticism and then recycled as reflections or commentaries on the fictional world of the new film" ("Future" 243). Soderbergh has repeatedly acknowledged the incorporation of other movies into his own, comparing the slow pacing in *Sex, Lies, and Videotape* to Wim Wenders's *Wings of Desire* (1987) and Francis Ford Coppola's *The Conversation* (1974), explaining the expressionism in *Kafka* as indebted to Fritz Lang and its cymbalum score by Cliff Martinez as influenced by the zither music in Carol Reed's *The Third Man* (1949), and describing *King of the Hill* as referencing Francois Truffaut's *Four Hundred Blows* (1959) (Kaufman 22, 50, 54, 62).

The Underneath combines elements of the noir film it remade—Robert Siodmack's 1946 crime story *Criss Cross*—with an Antonioni-like use of color to portray a protagonist disconnected from the world around him. Needing money after the box-office disappointment of his two previous films, Soderbergh initially took on the job of writing a straightforward thriller script for Universal but wound up keeping only two aspects of Siodmack's film: the idea of a man returning home to face a troubled past, and a scene in a hospital after a botched robbery. During the writing process Soderbergh realized that "there were certain elements in the script that were particular to me, and I wasn't at all sure that a third party would know what I had in mind. So I called Universal to tell them that I was planning to direct it myself" (Kaufman 70).

The Underneath tells the story of Michael (Peter Gallagher), a compulsive gambler who returns home for his mother's wedding three years after running away from gambling debts, only to be drawn by his attraction to his former wife, Rachel (Alison Elliot), into a disastrous robbery with her new husband, Tommy Dundee (William Fichtner). Except for that narrative starting point and the common noir theme of destructive desire—summed up by the scene of Michael hospitalized after being shot in the robbery—Soderbergh introduces a whole new set of narrative and formal choices. These include a complex temporal structure, suburban mise-en-scène, and stylized color to represent the world of the film as an expression of Michael's alienation and the emotionally destructive effects of his bad choices. Soderbergh referred to this alteration of the visual conventions of noir when he stated, "I told my collaborators: no wet pavement, no huge shadows, no hats, no smoke. That's not what I was looking for. So we spent our time talking about colors and space" (Kaufmann 72).

The banal mise-en-scène, the stultifying job Michael held selling sporting goods before he left, and working as an armored-car driver with his new father-in-law Ed (Paul Dooley) after his return help explain his alienation and disconnection from the world and people around him. As a tongue-in-cheek reference to Michael's unease, we see him reading self-help books with titles like *Self-Esteem: A User's Guide* and *Say Hello to Yourself* as he waits for Rachel to call or for the heist to happen. A green tint colors the present-tense sequences when the robbery takes place, suggesting his belief that quick money will solve his problems: a mistaken conviction that has taken Michael from gambling he couldn't afford to a botched armed robbery in which he is shot and Ed is killed. Such color symbolism is reinforced by a shot of the money tinted in the same shade of green as it being counted at the armored-car company just before the heist. A similar use of color functions in the shades of blue in stained glass and on the walls in Michael's mother's house, at the employee lounge of the armored-car company, inside the house he shared with Rachel when they were married, and that diffuse the early evening light as he and his ex-wife meet secretly to plot the renewal of their relationship. As green implies a hope that money will bring the meaning his life lacks, these shades of blue express the depressed emotions that his bad choices create for Michael and those close to him who occupy these spaces.

The Underneath failed to earn back even its $6.5 million production budget. While *Kafka* and *King of the Hill* may have put off audiences with their unresolved social conflicts and emphasis on the violence of inequality and oppression, the stylized use of color and the fragmented narrative chronology in *The Underneath* probably confused them. Soderbergh has acknowledged that "even my film crew didn't understand" the story. James Naremore points to the ambiguity that resulted from Soderbergh's modification of the noir original: "Throughout, *The Underneath* keeps its audience slightly off balance, joining the conventions of historical film noir with the more complex modernism of a New Wave director like Alain Resnais" (*More Than Night* 270).

Following the commercial disappointments of *Kafka, King of the Hill,* and *The Underneath,* in 1996 Soderbergh returned to Baton Rouge to direct and star in *Schizopolis,* made on a $250,000 budget with a skeleton cast and crew of friends and family. Although he credits this bare-bones film with giving him the opportunity to move away from the overly studied, formalistic approach that culminated in *The Underneath* in favor of the greater energy and spontaneity of a guerilla shooting style—an approach he would later employ in *Traffic, Full Frontal, Bubble, Che,* and *The Girlfriend Experience*—*Schiziopolis* was never released in theaters and brought his career back to square one. In May 1996, Soderbergh observed that neither *Schizopolis* nor *Gray's Anatomy*—another low-budget film he made that same year for the Independent Film Channel featuring the monologues of the performance artist Spalding Gray—ever "once appeared on *Variety's* weekly list of the top fifty or so grossing films. When you consider that films nestled at the bottom of the list are grossing as little as five or ten thousand dollars per week, you realize what an accomplishment this is" (Soderbergh 36). His sense of humor had survived intact, but Soderbergh was clearly dissatisfied by the binary choice between Hollywood and the obscurity of small-budget independent film. Writing a few months later, he stated that "this road . . . leads nowhere. . . . But what's the alternative? Go back and make stupid Hollywood movies? Or fake highbrow movies with people who would be as cynical about hiring me to make a 'smart' movie as others are when they hire the latest hot action director to make some blastfest?" (88–89).

Soderbergh's response to this impasse was to create a hybrid brand of filmmaking that gave him the commercial viability to continue directing and preserved a large measure of creative control, while at the same time reaffirming his reputation as a filmmaker dedicated to the social impact of movies, knowledgeable of the medium's history, and yet open to innovation. His opportunity to move in this direction came in 1997, when the chairman of Universal, Casey Silver, supported him for the job of directing a George Clooney and Jennifer Lopez vehicle based on Elmore Leonard's novel *Out of Sight.* Coming soon after the success of another Leonard adaptation, *Get Shorty* (1995), Paul Malcolm described Soderbergh's work on the film as "a particularly uncharacteristic capitulation to industry trends" (Kaufman 111). The earnings expectations created by the success of *Get Shorty,* a script in place when he came onboard, and a production budget bigger than that of his six previous films combined pushed Soderbergh outside what he called the "art-house ghetto" that had left him as frustrated as his alienated protagonists (Andrew, interview in this volume). While *Out of Sight* demonstrated Soderbergh's ability to make movies for a larger audience, it also offered him a chance to infuse that film, and the three other big-budget commercial successes he would direct in the next four years, with the social awareness and formal flair that characterize his earlier work. Looking back on this transitional period five years later, after the critical and commercial success of *Erin Brockovich, Traffic,* and *Ocean's Eleven* had validated his choice, Soderbergh explained the new direction his films had taken: "'It makes sense when you consider that the independent movement has been swallowed up by the studios, that I'd inevitably be some sort of hybrid. Maybe I was acting preemptively when I decided . . . to move toward the middle, because I don't know that I had a career . . . anymore'" (qtd. in Biskind 416).

However, not all of Soderbergh's films since *Out of Sight* have been hybridized in this way. Protected by his commercial successes, he has returned to the experimentation, strong stylization, and alienated characters of his first six films in *Bubble, Che,* and *The Girlfriend Experience,* which used nonprofessional actors, and, along with *Full Frontal,* employed digital video and improvisatory performance. *Solaris* and *The Good German* feature Clooney and *Full Frontal* includes Julia Roberts playing very unstarlike characters without unified or empowered identities. Soderbergh's choice to alternate between movies driven by his "personal preoccupations" and more broadly appealing films demonstrates that creativity and reaching an audience are not always mutually exclusive goals but in fact can be interdependent. Because of this earnings success (*Erin Brockovich, Traffic,* and the three *Ocean's* films have combined to generate over one and a half billion dollars in revenues worldwide), Soderbergh has enjoyed more creative control with his less commercial films.

In pursuing this strategy, Soderbergh has traded box-office hits for less profitable films with both Universal and Warner Brothers. While *Out of Sight* lost money for Universal in 1998, it demonstrated his skill with genre and stars, and that studio's faith in Soderbergh was rewarded with over $250 million in earnings from *Erin Brockovich* two years later. Soderbergh created a similar reciprocal relationship at Warner Brothers by generating huge profits from the *Ocean's* series, and in return the studio paid for his omnibus film *Eros*, with Michelangelo Antonioni and Wong Kar-wai, in 2004 and *The Good German* in 2006, both of which didn't make back their production budgets.

Besides using this quid-pro-quo strategy for his own films, Soderbergh has acted as a producer in support of other directors' "independent" projects. In 1999, he and George Clooney formed Section Eight, a production company set up to give filmmakers protection from a studio system increasingly guided by expectations of blockbuster profits and therefore wary of complex stories based in social realities. With the hope that Soderbergh and Clooney might produce "Oscar cachet," Warner Brothers agreed to provide a million-dollar budget for overhead and the use of Jack Warner's old office on their lot with the understanding that Soderbergh would have final cut and Section Eight would "make films as cheaply as possible in exchange for minimal creative interference" (McLean).

Section Eight delivered on its promise by producing a number of critically acclaimed and mostly smaller-budgeted films, including Todd Haynes's *Far from Heaven* (2002); Christopher Nolan's *Insomnia* (2002); Clooney's *Good Night, and Good Luck* (2005), which received six Academy Award nominations; Stephen Gaghan's *Syriana* (2005), for which Clooney won the Oscar for Best Supporting Actor; and Tony Gilroy's *Michael Clayton* (2007). The enormous profits from the three *Ocean's* films protected the less profitable Section Eight projects, but Soderbergh and Clooney also reduced risk by cutting their producer's fees, which they often put back into other projects, and by keeping budgets small. By March 2007, however, Soderbergh and Clooney closed Section Eight, having decided that the "crushing demand of studio meetings, correspondence, and project development" was becoming too much of a distraction from their own films (Holson 1). Soderbergh has continued to support other filmmakers, most notably helping to pay for the restoration and re-release in 2007 of Charles Burnett's film about the Los Angeles ghetto of Watts, *Killer of Sheep* (1977). Burnett's film had never been shown theatrically because of the cost of music rights, but in sixteen-millimeter format it had earned inclusion in the National Film

Registry and was selected by the National Society of Film Critics as one of the "Hundred Essential Films" of all time. But Soderbergh's strategy of directing profitable films that allow him to direct or produce less commercial projects has limits. In June 2009, Sony Pictures pulled the plug one week before shooting was scheduled to begin on *Moneyball*, a film starring Brad Pitt that Soderbergh was set to direct based on Michael Lewis's 2003 book about the Oakland Athletics general manager Billy Beane and his innovative methods of assessing player talent. Amy Pascal, the co-chair of Sony, stopped the fifty-eight-million-dollar project after reading Soderbergh's rewrite of the script. She was concerned that it would be too documentary in style and, compounded by the limited global appeal of baseball films, unlikely to return the studio's investment. *Moneyball* was later revived at Columbia with Bennett Miller directing a script rewritten by Aaron Sorkin and Steve Zaillian.

With Sony, Soderbergh didn't have the same kind of track record he had relied on with Universal and Warner Brothers. His involvement in *Moneyball* was based more on his relationship with Pitt and the assumption that it would be "unusual to see a studio step off a film to which a superstar like Pitt is firmly committed" (Bart and Fleming). Nonetheless, Pascal decided that *Moneyball* was too much of a risk under the strong pressures of a down economy. The *Los Angeles Times* reported that Sony's film-division sales had fallen 30 percent in the second quarter of 2009, during the time when Pascal pulled the plug on Soderbergh's version of *Moneyball* (Pham).

Chuck Klienhans has written that independent film "has always been a relational term, not an opposition" to Hollywood (308). Soderbergh's films exemplify this observation, sometimes closer and sometimes farther away from commercial Hollywood moviemaking in their style and content. His early films, like *Sex, Lies, and Videotape*, *Kafka*, and *The Underneath*, as well as more recent movies, such as *Full Frontal*, *Solaris*, *Bubble*, *The Good German*, *Che*, and *The Girlfriend Experience*, fit into the category of independent cinema as defined by an emphasis on characters whose alienation is communicated by a combination of realism and stylized form—a response to what King calls the "rarity" of "challenging perspectives on social issues" in Hollywood films (*American Independent* 2). These smaller films have also benefited from the forces that sustain independent cinema: home viewing, the aesthetic possibilities of inexpensive digital video, the decline of foreign film in the United States, the exposure made possible by festivals like Sundance, Tribeca, and Cannes, and the interest of studios in niche audiences once their commercial potential had been demonstrated. However, even Soderbergh's bigger-budget and more profitable films rely on some of the same tendencies, complicating the definition of "independent film" and supporting King's statement that Soderbergh's career demonstrates "the richness of the seam that can be mined in the area between Hollywood and the indie sector" (*American Independent* 262).

Remade by Steven Soderbergh: *The Underneath, Traffic, Ocean's Eleven, Solaris*

Four of Soderbergh's films are remakes of earlier movies or television programs consistent with his efforts to balance commercial and creative considerations. They exemplify the tendency in contemporary Hollywood to presell, in other words generating profits by recycling stories that have already demonstrated their marketability. Yet remakes have also allowed Soderbergh to accept the aesthetic challenge that Thomas Leitch describes when he says about the successful remake: "[T]he original film was outstanding—otherwise why bother to remake it at all?—yet the remake [must be] better still" (142). Understood this way, remakes fit with Soderbergh's use of allusion to appropriate and refashion narrative and formal elements from other films.

Such creative use of allusion and the remake responds to David Bordwell's idea of "belatedness": the anxiety of influence filmmakers feel with the entire history of cinema to measure themselves against (*Way Hollywood* 23). Although he didn't go to film school, Soderbergh is part of a generation of directors who have had access to film education through home video and DVD. His use of allusion and remakes demonstrates his knowledge of film history and ingratiates him with those in the audience who recognize the use of earlier films and therefore are made to feel like privileged insiders, creating what Bordwell calls "a pop connoisseurship that demands film references as part of the pleasures of moviegoing" (25).

The danger of such a film education for a director is that, the more one knows about movies, the higher the self-imposed standard to do something innovative. Bordwell sums up this burden when he poses the question: "With your career wholly in your own hands, facing the competition of past and present, how could you achieve something distinctive?" (*Way Hollywood* 23).

Like his adoption and modification of genre in films like *Kafka, The Underneath, Out of Sight, The Limey,* and *Ocean's Eleven,* Soderbergh uses allusion and remakes to attract audiences with the familiar but also to take advantage of the assumption that the invocation of earlier movies gives him license to modify them. Genre confirms audience expectations as to what kind of film they are watching, but it also risks boring viewers by simply recycling conventions. Soderbergh responds to this problem in *Kafka* by undermining the assumption of individual agency common to the biopic; in *Out of Sight,* he reverses the gender of the investigative protagonist and the sexually alluring but dangerous object of that search by making Jennifer Lopez the federal agent and Clooney the *homme fatale.* In his first remake, *The Underneath,* subjective narration and a mise-en-scène more reliant on suburban banality and the symbolic use of color than chiaroscuro and urban mean streets refashion Siodmack's noir story into an art film. Similarily, *The Limey* starts with the conventional premise of a revenge story in which, as Nicole Rafter describes the genre, "the outsider . . . is less interested in upholding a principle than in settling a personal grudge" (194). However, Soderbergh uses discontinuity editing to represent the memories and thought patterns of the Terence Stamp protagonist to demonstrate the incongruity between his plan for revenge and the past mistakes in his relationship with his daughter that are another source of his emotional pain.

Viewed from a commercial perspective, Soderbergh's second remake, *Traffic,* appears to have been motivated by a common pattern in Hollywood of redoing foreign films that have had limited distribution so as to increase their audience and profitability with the addition of bigger production budgets, increased marketing, and wider release. The model for *Traffic* was a 1990 BBC miniseries, *Traffik,* that was shown on public television in the United States. Rather than simply repackaging the British miniseries for a larger audience, however, Soderbergh adjusted its analysis of the international business of illegal drugs to show their impact on Mexico and the United States.

To achieve this shift, the producer Laura Bickford, the screenwriter Steven Gaghan, and Soderbergh changed the setting from the original BBC production's focus on Pakistan to Mexico; at the time the film was made, most of the illegal drugs entering the United States were coming through its southern border. *Traffic* shows that stimulating the drug trade has been a side effect of the 1993 North American Free Trade Agreement (NAFTA), which made the borders more porous and, with the removal of tariffs protecting small farmers in Mexico and the construction of *maquilladora* factories that undercut industrial production in the United States, increased the attraction of the drug economy for those displaced by globalization in both countries. Commenting on the impact of NAFTA, Jeff Faux has written that "on both sides of the U.S.-Mexico border, labor market competition has kept wages down. . . . By wiping out small Mexican farms that could not compete with heavily subsidized U.S. agribusiness, NAFTA also expanded the pool of unemployed young people that provides the narco-traffickers with recruits" (16, 18). The idea that legitimate work is a less viable alternative to the illegal drug economy is emphasized repeatedly in *Traffic*: Mexican soldiers protect the cartels, Benicio Del Toro's Tijuana cop earns only $316 per month, and the incentives for young African American dealers in inner-city Cincinnati are described by one character as "an unbeatable market force . . . you can go out on the street and make five hundred dollars in two hours." Scenes set in Mexico show men transporting drugs who exemplify how, in the era of "free trade," with the loss of government crop subsidies and the competition of transnational corporations, in the words of Curtis Marez, "local economies in Mexico . . . provide . . . few opportunities for survival other than drug production" (6).

One narrative strand in *Traffic* directly refers to the impact of globalization on the illegal drug trade. After he is arrested for selling narcotics to two undercover San Diego cops, Eduardo Ruiz (Miguel Ferrer) tells the officers questioning him that the dealer he works for gave up importing strawberries because drugs were more profitable and berates the police for the futility of their efforts. Ruiz chides them: "NAFTA makes things even more difficult for you, because the border's disappearing." While most of the U.S. government's efforts against drugs depicted in the film emphasize such failed interdiction, *Traffic* also demonstrates the importance of addressing the strong demand in the United States by highlighting the addiction of middle-class teenagers in suburban Cincinnati. The film implies that the escape of drug use is a response to the pressure these young people face to achieve as their parents have and to maintain their social and economic privilege in an increasingly competitive, globalized world. This alienation is made evident in the scene in which Caroline (Erika Christensen), the sixteen-year-old daughter of the U.S. drug czar Robert Wakefield (Michael Douglas), speaks to a social worker (Viola Davis) after she and her friends have been arrested for drug possession:

SOCIAL WORKER: In school?
CAROLINE: Yes.
SOCIAL WORKER: Private?
CAROLINE: Yeah.
SOCIAL WORKER: How are your grades?
CAROLINE: Third in my class . . . I get all A's.
SOCIAL WORKER: What else do you do?
CAROLINE: I'm a National Merit finalist . . . math team, Spanish club, vice president of my class . . . volleyball team.
SOCIAL WORKER: Do you want to tell me what you're doing here, Caroline?

From the social worker's perspective, Caroline's achievement in school should prevent the lack of hope that is often a cause of drug use, yet the teen's weary tone and depressed body language as she lists her accomplishments suggest that such intense pressure to achieve—and her view that hard work only leads to the unhappy, money- and status-driven lives of her parents—explain her desire to escape by getting high.

Soderbergh used handheld camera, available light, and the appearance of improvisational performance in an attempt to present a realistic story about illegal drugs. He prepared by analyzing two political films made in such a realist style, *Battle of Algiers* (1966) and *Z* (1969)—both of which he describes as having "that great feeling of things that are caught, instead of staged, which is what we were after" (Kaufman 158). The complexity of multiple storylines and an ensemble cast came from the BBC miniseries, which the critic Julie Salamon pointed out when she wrote that "both are layered works, cross-cutting among multiple scenarios, each intended to illuminate yet another ruthless and Byzantine aspect of the international drug business."

Soderbergh also retained from the BBC series the story about the addicted daughter of a high government official responsible for fighting illegal drugs to emphasize the importance of addressing the causes of addiction. Yet while the British production had room for long statements about the value of treatment, Soderbergh's film, with less than half the screen time, had to make more efficient use of a scene on a government jet in which Michael Douglas's drug czar, after his staff shows a lack of ideas, asks angrily, "Why is there no one from treatment on this plane?" The question fits with Marez's critical characterization of U.S. drug policy as "focused on military and police actions at the relative expense of education and treatment" (4).

Although *Traffic* emphasizes economic inequalities exacerbated by globalization and government ineffectiveness as determining factors in the problem of illegal drugs, Soderbergh ultimately chose to preserve the movie's commercial viability by avoiding the more explicit social critique of a film like *Battle of Algiers*—even if its real locations and handheld camerawork were a stylistic influence—in favor of staying within the parameters of the Hollywood social-problem film. As Peter Roffman and Jim Purdy point out, the social-problem film has to "deal with controversial matters very much on the surface . . . with discretion" (7). *Traffic* ends with a resolution made up of individualized responses: Wakefield gives up his high-profile position to pay greater attention to his daughter, and the principled cops played by Benecio Del Toro and Don Cheadle keep doing their jobs, despite the murders of their partners, out of commitment to their disadvantaged communities. As a result, the early concerns of Barry Diller, the head of USA Films, which financed *Traffic*, that "a $50 million art film, about drugs, [with] sequences in Spanish . . . [and] with so many actors you needed a scorecard" would not succeed commercially proved unfounded (Biskind 379). By offsetting its narrative and stylistic complexity with the appeal of stars (Michael Douglas, Catherine Zeta-Jones, Benicio Del Toro, and Don Cheadle), good reviews, and Oscar nominations for Best Supporting Actor (Del Toro), Best Director, and Best Picture, *Traffic* grossed over two hundred million dollars.

With an even bigger budget and lineup of stars than in *Traffic*, Soderbergh's third remake, *Ocean's Eleven*, marked his strongest move in the direction of commercial cinema. His own proclamation that it was "just a big windup toy" he was nonetheless happy to make "because entertainment is a good thing" fit the expectation that marketing big-budget movies requires portraying them as not challenging to viewers (Andrew, interview in this volume). Yet, if one considers that Soderbergh changed the Rat Pack original to allow eleven robbers to get away with $150 million, foregrounded the aesthetic nature of the heist, and justified the crime by vilifying the casino owner, Terry Benedict (Andy Garcia), his *Ocean's Eleven* becomes an allegory of the growing gulf of class difference in supply-side America and the role of the movies in affirming or critiquing it. By changing the ending to contrast with the Production Code–regulated conclusion of the 1960 original, in which the thieves lose the stolen money when it inadvertently burns up in the coffin where it had been hidden, Soderbergh refers to the earlier movie through what Noel Carroll has called an "expressive device": an alteration of the original story that indicates the remake's different interpretation of the meaning of the robbery ("Future of Allusion" 242).

Although the fantasy of stealing $150 million cut eleven ways is about as much of a viable response to the problem of wealth inequality in America as buying a lottery ticket, Soderbergh's *Ocean's Eleven* is less a real-world strategy than a symbolic reaction to what the economist Edward Wolff describes as "a clear shift in national income away from labor and towards capital . . . since the early 1980s," and the role of entertainment in distracting the vast majority of Americans disadvantaged by that change (22).

Terry Benedict embodies what contemporary Las Vegas represents: the consolidation of wealth in American society. The casino where the robbery takes place, the Bellagio, and the Strip's other new megacasinos with international themes, were built in the 1990s by entrepreneurs such as Steve Wynn (the model for Benedict) with junk bonds like those used by corporate raiders to acquire companies and eliminate jobs (Denton and Morris 355). With its art gallery and upscale restaurants, the Bellagio is part of a diversification strategy in Las Vegas to include nongaming revenue, yet the appeal of such amenities, like gambling itself, is fueled by how both offer consumers escape from the reality of diminished opportunities for upward mobility within an American economy of stagnant wages, outsourcing, and layoffs. Jacob S. Hacker points out that "between 1979 and 2003 the average income of the richest Americans more than doubled after adjusting for inflation, while that of middle-class Americans increased by only around 15 percent" (12). Richard McGowan has documented that during the same period, revenue from gambling in the United States exploded from one billion to over seventy billion dollars. Within a postindustrial, globalized economy, gambling increasingly appears to offer the best way, in the words of Robert Goodman, "to get ahead . . . in a world where work no longer seems reliable" (qtd. in Lears 325).

With eleven major characters to set up, the exposition in *Ocean's Eleven* is by necessity economical. Nonetheless, each of the robbers comes with some indication that they embody the disaffection created by the increasing division of American society into haves and have-nots, whether it be a criminal past, lack of work, or entrapment in a job in which they are unappreciated or unrewarded. Even the bankroll behind the job, the former casino owner Reuben Tishkoff (Elliot Gould), wants revenge against a new economy in which corporate moguls like Benedict can use the financial muscle of consolidation to push him out. With his three casinos and hundreds of millions in assets, Benedict refers to the horizontally integrated corporate control of mass entertainment; the eleven thieves succeed in robbing him using storytelling, performative, and guerilla-technological skills that symbolize the independent-film sensibility. Soderbergh exemplifies this ethos in the movie's avoidance of violent spectacle in favor of good writing, skilled acting, and subordination of star power within an ensemble story. Early in *Ocean's Eleven*, Soderbergh makes reference to this independent aesthetic. After the opening scene, in which Clooney is interviewed and released from prison by a parole board, the next sequence begins with a helicopter shot across water, tilting up to show the bright lights of Atlantic City. The helicopter shot and tilt up imitate the similar imagery and camera movement used in opening titles to identify films distributed by Miramax, the company most responsible for making independent film commercially viable, which is in part what *Ocean's Eleven* also achieves.

While Soderbergh conceals the social commentary and self-reflexivity of *Ocean's Eleven* behind its expensive production values and genre familiarity, his fourth remake, *Solaris,* was a tougher sell because it more radically upset audience expectations for science fiction and a George Clooney star vehicle. Instead of battling spaceships, lightsabers, or aliens emerging from the chests of crew members, *Solaris* is an introspective, character-based film with a complex narrative structure and foregrounded form. But even those aspects of *Solaris* that were determined by commercial considerations—the presence of Clooney; James Cameron as the film's producer; the reduction of Andrei Tarkovsky's 165-minute original to an efficient ninety-nine; and the displacement of what Jonathan Rosenbaum calls the 1972 Soviet film's "meditative poetry" on art and science by a love story about a psychiatrist, Chris Kelvin (Clooney), sent to a space station where a nearby planet has the power to bring his dead wife Rheya (Natascha McElhone) back to him—don't alter its fundamental focus on an expressive minimalism (Rosenbaum).

Despite flashbacks of Chris and Rheya early in their relationship that emphasize Clooney's charm, humor, and physical appeal—including a brief nude shot of him—*Solaris* is generally slow-moving, without much dialogue or action for long stretches, as if to emphasize the power of Kelvin's subjective experience. *Solaris* also strongly returns to the formalist emphasis of Soderbergh's "smaller" films. After the pop/jazz/funk pastiche of David Holmes's score, which matched the fast-paced narrative in *Ocean's Eleven,* Soderbergh chose the haunting Brian Eno–inspired synthesizer music of his longtime collaborator Cliff Martinez to communicate the feeling of isolation in outer space. Similarly, Jonathan Romney has suggested that the production designer Philip Messina's careful attention to the futuristic decor of the space station makes as much of an impression as the narrative itself: "[T]extures and elegant details . . . show that the accoutrements of lifestyle follow humanity even unto the depths of the galaxy: you may find yourself remembering the film for a certain metallic sheen on Clooney's pillow, or the strange ice tray edging around his bed" (17).

Like Soderbergh's other experiences with stylized alienation, *Solaris* failed to reach much of an audience. Perhaps he thought Clooney's star appeal and Cameron's imprimatur would offset the movie's formal and thematic challenges. However, in a year in which the two top earning sci-fi films, George Lucas's *Star Wars: Episode II* and Steven Spielberg's *Minority Report,* used digital imagery and spectacular violence to earn

$450 million dollars together, the deemphasis on action and special effects in favor of allusion—via experimental music, deliberate pacing, and an ambiguous ending—to 1960s "art cinema appropriation of the [sci-fi] genre" by the likes of François Truffaut and Stanley Kubrick put *Solaris* at a commercial disadvantage (Romney 17).

Regardless of the obscurity of *The Underneath* and *Solaris*, taken as a whole Soderbergh's four remakes demonstrate his interest in reconciling creative and commercial motivations. As production and marketing budgets have pushed the average cost for a Hollywood film higher and higher, studios are increasingly interested in remakes with "presold" stories that audiences know and have proven they will pay to see. The assumption is not necessarily that the remake will improve creatively on the original film but rather that it can match or exceed its earnings. While *The Underneath* and *Solaris* were too focused on subjective realities communicated through stylized form to appeal to many viewers, *Ocean's Eleven's* updating of the conventional crime film to present a fast-moving and stylish critique of the consolidation of wealth in American society and *Traffic's* use of an ensemble cast and a realist style to describe the complexities of the business of illegal drugs in the age of globalization both show that important issues and commercial appeal can coexist in remakes.

Moreover, Soderbergh's use of remakes and allusion represents a broader interest in refashioning established cinematic forms that is one of the larger tendencies of his movies. In *Sex, Lies, and Videotape* he helped define independent cinema as a larger part of the cable and home-video market by alluding to, but ultimately subverting, the voyeuristic assumptions of the softcore films that had become an established staple for those outlets during the 1980s. Likewise, *King of the Hill* complicates another genre that was becoming important in the age of home viewing, the kid pic, by adding an unflinching depiction of the brutal effects of poverty, especially on children who have no responsibility for their economic status. *The Underneath* and *Solaris* substantially reshaped the films they were based upon; along with *The Limey*, they offer genre movies redone with a large dose of art-film subjective narration. *Erin Brockovich* and *Traffic* present complex stories about social problems in a realist style but also reached large audiences by doubling as star vehicles. With *Full Frontal*, Soderbergh remade *Sex, Lies, and Videotape*—using videotape. He has stated that the later film has the look he would have used for his debut had digital technology been available at that time (Taylor 1). *Full Frontal* also revisits the attempt in *Sex, Lies, and Videotape* to record the zeitgeist of a generation, although when it came out in 2001 not much had changed since 1989: both stories show characters with a strong sense of entitlement and the emotional fallout from their selfish actions. What was different was Soderbergh's approach to realism: the use of the actual locations remained from the earlier film, but the long takes and slow tracking shots of *Sex, Lies, and Videotape* gave way to handheld digital-video imagery.

Ocean's *Twelve* is the one film in which Soderbergh didn't pursue either an art film or hybrid aesthetic. Instead, he seemed content to extend the commercial success of *Ocean's Eleven* by following the conventional pattern for a sequel of offering viewers a recycling of the experience of the popular first film—without the social commentary. *Ocean's Twelve* repeats a number of formal aspects from *Ocean's Eleven*, emphasizing the same realistic look, using actual locations—Amsterdam and Italy rather than Las Vegas—handheld camerawork, and the appearance of available light, energized by fast-paced cutting set to another David Holmes up-tempo score.

Ocean's Twelve, like *Ocean's Eleven*, also continues to favor characterization over plot, again distinguishing the title character and his crew through their ability to strategize, perform, and deceive, often with a skillful use of language, and their mastery of high technology. The central heist in the story—of a jewel-encrusted Fabergé egg from a Rome museum—functions to reiterate this emphasis on characterization; we learn at the end of the film that the robbery is an elaborate ruse. Danny Ocean and company have already swapped it for a replica before it is put on display, making the robbery that is central to the movie's plot just a distraction. Ocean's wife Tess (Julia Roberts) had become the twelfth member of the crew by impersonating Julia Roberts to gain special access to the museum. But just as the theft using Tess/Roberts and a sophisticated high-tech hologram doesn't really matter within the story, likewise the crime itself and the self-reflexive dimension of Roberts's contribution lack the subtext of social and cultural critique found in the use of genre and stars in the 2001 remake. While robbing the three Vegas casinos was an act of class warfare, and the use of an independent aesthetic to do so attacked corporate entertainment, stealing in *Ocean's*

Twelve is simply to pay Benedict back the money taken from him, as if the robbery in the first film was just a mistake.

Ocean's Twelve is therefore not about redistributing wealth but rather consolidating it. Even the few ways in which the sequel adds new elements appear calculated to increase profit. Catherine Zeta-Jones as the Interpol investigator Isabel Lahiri and Bruce Willis in a cameo role add two more bankable stars to the cast, and the beautiful European locales and David Holmes's addition of a world-music dimension to the score help *Ocean's Twelve* take better aim at overseas markets.

While *Ocean's Twelve* follows the formula for a sequel by offering the audience a replay of what worked in *Ocean's Eleven*, *Ocean's Thirteen* returns to Las Vegas and remakes the 2001 film by reconstructing the story of the crew of thieves outwitting a greedy power player with violent tendencies, in this case Al Pacino rather than Andy Garcia. In *Ocean's Thirteen,* Clooney and his crew team up again to defend Reuben after he is ruthlessly cut out of a development deal on a new Strip hotel and casino by Willy Bank (Pacino). The Pacino character's last name implies how he stands for a pervasive problem of greed beyond his own economic interests, while Ocean and his crew embody the higher values of friendship and creativity by putting all their money—along with another thirty-six million dollars borrowed from Terry Benedict—into an elaborate plan, again relying on the performance and technology skills that have characterized them throughout the trilogy, to sabotage the earnings of Bank's hotel/casino.

Pacino's presence seems to have also inspired Soderbergh's interest in allusion, as several lines borrow verbatim from *The Godfather* (1972). When Clooney approaches Bank to discuss the dispute with Reuben, he quotes from the restaurant scene in which Pacino's Michael Corleone tells Salozzo before shooting him, "What I want, what's most important to me. . . ." Later, when Reuben awakens from the heart-attack-induced coma he suffers after Bank muscles him out, he speaks to Danny and Rusty in the words of Marlon Brando's Don Corleone just out of bed after the attempt on his life: "I hear cars pulling in, I hear whispering conversations. . . . Why don't you tell me what everyone seems to know?"

Such allusion signals Soderbergh's intention to follow Francis Ford Coppola's lead in *The Godfather, Part II* of amplifying the political statement that had been obscured by the performances and genre action of the first film. In *Part II*, Coppola expanded his critique of the American political and economic system established in *The Godfather* by more overtly paralleling the Corleone mafia family with "legitimate" business and government figures through the senator who tries to shake down Michael as he invests in Las Vegas, and particularly by the scene showing Pacino meeting in Cuba with representatives of major American corporations such as AT&T and United Fruit. Similarly, in *Ocean's Eleven*, Andy Garcia, who played Sonny Corleone's son in *The Godfather, Part III*, reinvokes the idea that "legitimate" corporate leaders act criminally to gain and preserve their vast wealth. But in *Ocean's Thirteen* it is the actor who was the head of the mafia family in Coppola's films (Pacino) who makes even more explicit threats of criminal violence in the service of business. Bank gives Reuben the choice of signing over his interest in the hotel/casino or being thrown off its roof.

Besides how the allusions to *The Godfather* series help augment the criminal evil of the story's businessman bad guy, Soderbergh in *Ocean's Thirteen* also gives greater direct representation to the interests of working people. In several scenes we see the Malloy brothers, first Virgil and later Turk, involved in a successful strike at the dice factory in Ciudad Juarez that supplies Bank's casino. While the strike scenes are played for laughs, and Soderbergh makes gentle fun of traditional labor slogans— the workers "want bread *and* roses"—and of their violent face-offs with Mexican riot police, the labor demands are described ($3.50 more per week, a 50 percent increase) in a tone of earnest outrage. Likewise, the movie's climactic scene of the successful manipulation of blackjack, dice, and roulette on the floor of Bank's casino to let all the gamblers take away big winnings creates a triumphant tone with split screens, fast editing, and energized music. Finally, to drive home the idea that the people have won this time, Ocean wraps up the film by orchestrating the donation of Terry Benedict's share in the scam to support a camp for foster kids.

Regardless of the lack of a consistent hybridization of art cinema and Hollywood genre film throughout the *Ocean's* series, underlying Soderbergh's use of allusion, stylization, social protest, stars, and continuity of form in his remake and its sequels are two unchanging assumptions: that movies invoke other movies as well as external realities, and that the value of this eclectic mixture lies in representing both.

Star Actors: Julia Roberts,
Michael Douglas, George Clooney

Soderbergh's films also remake the conventions of Hollywood cinema by being both character- and star-driven at the same time. The presence of George Clooney, Julia Roberts, Cate Blanchett, Brad Pitt, Michael Douglas, Benicio Del Toro, Matt Damon, and Catherine Zeta-Jones has undoubtedly helped him get his films made and seen, yet Soderbergh has modified the practice in Hollywood by which, in the words of Richard Maltby, "the commercial imperatives of the star system require that stars are always visible through their characters" (384). This modification has been achieved by harnessing the revenue potential of stars to get films on screens and therefore to audiences that might not otherwise see them, while also asking actors for performances that support complex characters and stories, often within ensemble casts.

The importance of stars in Hollywood filmmaking often results in what Barry King describes as a subordination of acting—the ability to "disappear into the part" and impersonate a fictional character—to "personification," which places "emphasis on what is unique to the actor, displacing emphasis from what an actor can do *qua* actor onto what actor *qua* person or biographical entity is" (168, 178). King views the Method style of acting, which asks for an expression of the actor's "'organic' self," as an adaptation of film performance to the need for stars, allowing bankable performers to present their personalities rather than having to become the character (179).

As with Soderbergh's modification of remakes to create room for his aesthetic and social concerns, the commercial security of working with high-profile actors, and their interest in demonstrating their acting skills by appearing in character-centered films under his direction, has allowed him to qualify this typical emphasis on personification. In describing the ways in which *Erin Brockovich* differs from the conventional big-budget Hollywood film, Soderbergh acknowledged the importance of having Julia Roberts—whose films had earned two billion dollars worldwide—in the lead role:

> *Erin Brockovich* . . . is an aggressively linear reality-based drama about
> a twice-divorced mother of three who is living at a very low-end income

level, who talks herself into a job answering the phone and ends up putting together a case against a large California utility company that results in the biggest direct-action lawsuit settlement in history. She's played by Julia Roberts—if you're trying to sneak something under the wire, by which I mean an adult, intelligent film with no sequel potential, no merchandising, no high concept, and no big hook, it's nice to have one of the world's most bankable stars sneaking under with you. (Kaufman 119)

As if to establish the commercial viability they bring to the films, Roberts in *Erin Brockovich*, Michael Douglas in *Traffic*, and George Clooney in *Solaris* and *The Good German* initially refer in their roles to the traits that made them stars. For example, Roberts's role foregrounds the unself-conscious sexuality associated with her since *Pretty Woman* (1990). Charlotte Brunsdon wrote about Roberts's character in that breakthrough performance: "Although Vivian is working as a prostitute for most of the film, the dominant presentation of her is as naturally not-a-hooker" (96). Brunsdon details how Vivian's care with money (she saves it for rent, while her roommate spends it on drugs), her seemingly natural laugh and smile, and her uncontrived use of her appearance and sexuality were all traits that endeared the character—and by extension, Roberts—to audiences. As Brunsdon puts it, "Even though Vivian works as a prostitute, she is unconscious of the power of her beauty. . . . She might be a hooker outside, but she's clean inside" (99).

This image of Roberts as sexualized but fundamentally moral and honest was further developed in roles after *Pretty Woman*. Contrary to what her biographer, James Spada, calls the "serial mankiller" label that came from tabloid coverage of her real-life relationships, even her characters in films such as *My Best Friend's Wedding* (1997) and *Runaway Bride* (1999), who initially appear to manipulate men, turn out to be honest and caring. In another film made just before *Erin Brockovich*, *Notting Hill* (1999), she plays a movie star based on her own career who by the end of the story displays the same warmth and genuineness. Such moral integrity and concern for others are the traits that Soderbergh uses to promote audience identification with Erin Brockovich and her cause; she succeeds in revealing Pacific Gas and Electric's legal responsibility for water contamination and helps hundreds of plaintiffs obtain compensation from the utility.

Good looks and compassion are traits that audiences associated with Roberts and that the real Erin Brockovich had used effectively in her legal work, creating a good fit between the star and the historical figure she plays. On several occasions in the story, Roberts's Erin uses low-cut tops and short skirts to disarm male characters, particularly the employee of the water board whose permission she needs to access documentation important to the case against Pacific Gas and Electric (PG&E). Moreover, it is only because Roberts's character contrasts herself to the lawyers who are primarily focused on their careers, and can convince the plaintiffs of her sincerity and concern for them, that they agree to join the class-action suit.

However, *Erin Brockovich* is a story about a complex legal case and the tragic impact of environmental contamination, so Roberts had to demonstrate a greater level of intelligence and verbal acuity, as well as more emotional depth, than in most of her previous roles. Because her stardom had been built on a combination of sexuality and down-to-earth warmth and directness, audiences may not have expected her to effectively play a role leading a legal case against a giant utility that requires the brains and toughness more characteristic of a Susan Sarandon or Kathy Bates. Besides the need for greater focus and resolve, Roberts also had to augment her unself-conscious sexuality and warmth, conveyed in the past through her vibrant smile, with quiet empathy for the victims. This emotional depth in Roberts's performance is best established in the scenes in which she talks with Donna (Marg Helgenberger), whose family has had numerous health problems as a result of contaminated water.

The conversations between the two women appear mostly in close-up and shot/reverse shot figures, with Erin initially asking a few questions and later presenting Donna with the painful truth of PG&E's role in her family's medical problems. For most of these scenes, Erin listens intently to Donna, with Roberts using her body, facial expression, and voice to convey the concern she feels. After explaining PG&E's contamination of the family's water in their second meeting, Erin watches, leaning forward and with her shoulders slumped, as Donna rushes outside to get her two daughters from the backyard pool. The two women's next meeting is prefaced by jump cuts linking Donna's husband throwing rocks at the nearby PG&E plant, screaming, and dropping to his knees in pain. In this exchange, Donna tells Erin about her recent cancer diagnosis and breaks down, pleading, "You've got to promise me we'll get them!" Soderbergh cuts to a close-up of Roberts, who, with moist eyes, nods shakily and responds quietly, "Yeah" (see figure 2).

In addition to such emotional empathy, Susannah Grant's script called on Roberts to display her character's intellectual ability by speaking large amounts of dialogue relating to the specifics of the case, as when she upstages the highly paid attorneys by demonstrating her ability to recall the names, family histories, and medical conditions of all 634 plaintiffs. Another exchange with the lead attorney refers to Erin's intelligence as well as her attractiveness. After she presents him with consent forms from all the plaintiffs and internal PG&E memoranda admitting culpability in poisoning groundwater, he asks incredulously, "How'd you do this?" Erin replies, "Seeing how I have no brains or law expertise . . . I just went out there and performed sexual favors." Her sarcastic response makes reference to the lawyer's assumptions that an uneducated, single mother would not possess such organizational and investigative skills, but also perhaps to the audience's surprise when Julia Roberts goes beyond the limitations of her star image to represent her character's intelligence.

Roberts's performance in *Erin Brockovich* draws on the sexuality and down-to-earth appeal of her star image but also conveys the commitment

Figure 2. Erin empathizes with Donna.

and intelligence of the title character in a manner consistent with the idea of impersonation favored by King. James Spada sums up how the resulting performance combines the two: "Typecast as a 'star performer,' someone whose personality and looks were more impressive and marketable than her dramatic abilities, and an actress who needed to be sunny (and grinning widely) . . . her performance in *Erin Brockovich*, although undeniably big on looks and personality, also gave her an opportunity to inhabit a character as she never had before, and to show a range of emotions" (361). Soderbergh similarly describes the balance of star appeal and the acting required of Roberts: "One of the reasons this was such a good part was that it played to all of her strengths, and yet there was something a little heavier at the center than she normally plays" (Grady).

Not only was *Erin Brockovich* based on the impressive true story of a single mother who played a major role in winning a $333 million class-action judgment, the film's importance was underlined by information from Los Angeles city records published in an article on the front page of the *Los Angeles Times* soon after its release. The *Times* story explains that the carcinogen at the center of the judgement, Chromium 6, was discharged for decades into the Los Angeles River (Blankstein A1). While many Hollywood social-problem films are heavy on populist melodrama and thin on the specifics of controversial issues, *Erin Brockovich* used Roberts's star power and nuanced performance to draw public attention to an important environmental problem. Soderbergh's film is mentioned in the concluding paragraph of the *Times* story, a clear indication that it contributed to the newspaper's interest in making this previously unpublished information public.

As with Julia Roberts in *Erin Brockovich*, Soderbergh has cast Michael Douglas and and George Clooney in roles that go beyond their star images. His reputation for successful collaboration with star actors served Soderbergh well in making *Traffic*, as Douglas accepted the use of a deglamorized visual style, with handheld camera and available light, as well as reduced screen time within an ensemble story involving thirteen major characters necessary to represent complex social, political, and economic issues that impact the flow of illegal drugs between Mexico and the United States. Soderbergh acted as his own cinematographer, filming most of *Traffic* with a small crew. Such a guerilla style allowed shooting to move quickly and actors to remain focused, helping Douglas maintain the emotional intensity needed for his character. Soderbergh explained: "There were a couple of key emotional scenes where we were moving so quickly that it enabled [Douglas] to stay right there, and there would be a break of two minutes between one angle and the next. I was really impressed, performance-wise, at how readily he fell into the low-key naturalistic approach that I was trying to maintain. It's not a movie-star performance" (Kaufman 144). The emotional intensity of such a character-based performance is increasingly visible as Douglas's Bob Wakefield learns more about how the "war on drugs" is mishandled by the Mexican and U.S. governments. The poise and self-assurance associated with Douglas's star persona erodes as Wakefield realizes the futility of his high-profile position—such as during the meeting on the plane, when none of his staff can address the issue of treatment—while he must simultaneously confront his daughter's addiction. When we first see Douglas, still working as a federal judge, he assertively corrects a defense attorney in a drug trial, and a short time later we hear him boasting to Caroline and his wife Barbara (Amy Irving) of his appointment as drug czar and "face time" with the president. These early scenes show the confidence and control that Douglas has displayed in roles from *Wall Street* (1987) to *The American President* (1995). Even in his well-known parts in *Fatal Attraction* (1987) and *Basic Instinct* (1992), in which that control is undermined, the narratives move toward its reassertion and the punishment of the female characters responsible for challenging it. Conversely, in *Traffic*, the addiction of Wakefield's daughter contributes to the subversion of his patriarchal control, and he responds to her need for him to play a more compromising, supportive role.

In one sequence that exemplifies how the Wakefield part asked Douglas to move beyond a starlike self-assurance and control and submerge himself in the character, he goes with Caroline's boyfriend Seth (Topher Grace) in search of his missing daughter to an inner-city Cincinnati neighborhood where the teenagers have bought drugs in the past. Their dealer (Vonte Sweet) threatens Wakefield with a gun and refuses to give him any information on the whereabouts of his daughter, leaving him so distraught that he can only react weakly to the circumstances in which his daughter's addiction has placed him. Although he eventually locates Caroline strung out in a cheap hotel, this experience makes clear to Wakefield the necessity of understanding the causes for her addiction.

He therefore regards as futile his position as a federal official leading a war on drugs that is almost exclusively focused on interdiction and prosecution, seeing it as tantamount to what he calls in his resignation speech "waging war on our own families."

But, as much as Douglas subordinates his star image to the Wakefield character, the prominence of his role within the story plays a major part in how its central issues get resolved. Richard Maltby has observed that "questions raised at the level of the plot can be resolved at the level of performance, as the audience's attention is displaced away from the issues at stake in the fiction onto the way in which stars exhibit themselves under the pressure of those issues" (387).

This displacement occurs in *Traffic*, as the political question at the center of the story—is the best response to the problem of illegal drugs interdiction of those who transport and sell them, or should we address the causes of demand as well?—gets resolved in favor of the latter through Wakefield's choice to give up his position leading U.S. government policy focused on law enforcement so as to help his daughter beat her addiction. As this choice occurs at the individual level of Douglas's performance, and is not presented as a change in U.S. government policy, Soderbergh is able to endorse the idea of treatment using the emotional appeal of a father's commitment to his daughter, without needing to make an overt ideological statement, thus exemplifying what Maltby calls the use of star performance "to exploit political subject matter without abandoning [a] commitment to entertainment" (387).

Like Roberts in *Erin Brockovich* and Douglas in *Traffic*, George Clooney in *Solaris* initially refers to his star image before modifying it to meet the needs of his character. Soon after his arrival on the space station, we see Kelvin's dreams about the early stages of his relationship with his wife Rheya in which the sense of humor and charm associated with Clooney are foregrounded. From the middle 1990s, when he gained attention for his role as Dr. Doug Ross in the highly rated television hospital drama *ER*, Clooney has frequently played attractive, charming—but transgressive—leads. This rebelliousness has been defined by criminal parts in films such as *Out of Sight*, *Three Kings* (1999), *O Brother, Where Art Thou?* (2000), and the *Ocean's* series, as well as through publicity about his bachelor lifestyle and political involvements.

However, in *Solaris*, Clooney's charm and confident self-assertion quickly disappear as Rheya materializes in his cabin on the space station where he has been sent to assess the psychological problems of the crew. Initially he can neither understand nor accept her presence, and his decision to expel her out into space only compounds the guilt and depression he feels from their past failed relationship and her suicide. Even in the happier flashback scenes, in which we see the couple falling in love and that seem to explain Kelvin's desire for her return, Soderbergh plants hints of the psychiatrist's inability to understand his wife. For the scene in which they first notice each other on a commuter train, the director had asked Natascha McElhone to choose a random prop to hold. McElhone selected a doorknob, a prop that Soderbergh describes as "open ended" in its meaning, and as we see it from the perspective of the Kelvin character, its indeterminacy foreshadows his subsequent confusion and impatience with her emotions when she becomes depressed (DVD commentary). Such a lack of understanding on the part of Clooney's character offsets the agency implied by his attractiveness and charm shown early in the relationship, as well as by his professional skill as a psychiatrist to solve the problems of the other personnel on the space station. His confusion sets Kelvin up instead to accept the solution to his emotional distress offered by Solaris, as it can materialize his desire and bring Rheya back to him. As another example of Soderbergh's tendency to offset the conventions of heroic agency with the character subjectivity of art cinema, Kelvin's choice to remain on Solaris because the planet can provide him with a second chance in his marriage is more an affirmation of the power of internal desire than the objective action that generally defines the performances of male star actors.

Clooney's roles in *Solaris* and *The Good German* fit the pattern that his career has taken toward balancing sexy, outlaw heroes with less glamorous parts in films such as *Syriana, Good Night, and Good Luck,* and *Michael Clayton,* in which larger forces complicate his characters' individual agency. As an acknowledgment of this more political dimension to his work, Clooney told an interviewer that Soderbergh sent him John Garfield films to watch to prepare for the role of Jake Geismer in the *The Good German* (Murray). Most relevant about Garfield for Clooney's role was the former's experience of paying a high price in his professional and personal life when he was blacklisted for his political beliefs. Based on Joseph Kanon's novel, *The Good German* tells a similar story of how the political pressures of the cold war neutralized Geismer's ability to fight for human rights. *The Good German* is therefore another of Soderbergh's films that alludes to earlier films and incorporates unconventional performances by star actors as a variation on the norms of Hollywood filmmaking. Employing the language of the high-concept pitch parodied by Robert Altman in *The Player* (1992), Cynthia Fuchs refers to the *Good German* as "*Double Indemnity* meets *Casablanca,*" implying the noir fatalism with which Soderbergh subverts the patriotic optimism of Michael Curtiz's 1942 film. In *Casablanca,* the previously noncommitted—"I stick my neck out for nobody"—Rick Blaine (Humphrey Bogart) reluctantly involves himself on behalf of his former love, Ilsa Lund (Ingrid Bergman), and her Resistance-leader husband, Victor (Paul Henreid), to help them escape the Nazis. *The Good German* sets up roughly the same narrative situation, as Geismer must decide whether to help Lena Brandt (Cate Blanchett) and her husband Emil (Christian Oliver) escape the dangers of postwar Berlin. Yet, in Soderbergh's film, self-interest overwhelms the larger good as it is defined by justice and the rule of law.

Unlike Ilsa, Lena is not torn between love for the American protagonist and the moral imperative of supporting a noble husband. Instead, she is simply a woman victimized by war, forced to prostitute herself to survive, and, worse yet, a self-proclaimed "Nazi Jew" who has betrayed twelve other Jews to the Gestapo to avoid a death camp. When Lena pulls a gun on Jake in a scene that recalls Ilsa's attempt to get letters of transit from Rick in *Casablanca,* it is to protect her own plan of escape, not to help her husband evade capture. And while Ilsa's love for Rick would never allow her to really shoot him, we can't be sure of Lena, since she has already killed Seargeant Tully (Tobey Maguire), another ex-lover who tried to get in the way of her escape.

If Bogart's Rick Blaine embodies the strong individual who stands for the heroic involvement of the United States in World War II to fight Nazi tryanny, in *The Good German* Americans are either ineffectual, like Geismer, or self-interested to the point of criminality. Congressman Breimer (Jack Thompson) and Colonel Muller (Beau Bridges) so much want to get the V2 missile designer Franz Bettman (David Willis) back to the United States to start making cold-war weapons systems that they'll lie about his Nazi past and kill anyone who tries to interfere. They therefore murder Emil Brandt, who has documents to prove that thirty thousand slave laborers died in Bettman's underground V2 factory. Tully, who works the black market with the hope of earning enough to escape Germany with Lena, is equally self-interested and almost as violent, if less sophisticated, prompting Cynthia Fuchs to describe him as representative of "the ugly American . . . mucking about in world affairs."

Clooney's presence in *The Good German* fits with Soderbergh's practice of exploiting star power, but, as in *Solaris*, together the director and actor deconstruct its superficial celebration of heroism in favor of more complex characterization. In contrast to Bogart's white tuxedo in *Casablanca* or the elegant suits of *Ocean's Eleven*, Clooney wears a standard-issue wool U.S. army uniform. Patches stitched on the breast and sleeve say "War Correspondent," as if, since his investigation is always a step behind the action throughout the film, we have to be reminded that the character has a profession he's capable of doing. As in *Good Night, and Good Luck* and *Syriana,* Clooney looks a little heavy and

Figure 3. Bandage as allusion
in *The Good German.*

tired, and such an appearance fits Jake, as he spends much of the film reacting too slowly and getting beaten up several times by those whose plans he tries to understand or interrupt. Even when Jake fights back, in the scene in which he kills an assassin sent by Muller to murder Emil, Geismer's success is only temporary, as Brandt stumbles out into a crowd where another hired killer finishes the job. Besides his contrastive reference to Bogart in *Casablanca*, the injuries Clooney gains as result of his beatings represented by the bandage on his ear set up a second allusion to define his character—to another noir investigator named Jake. Jack Nicholson's Jake Gittes in *Chinatown* (1975) also sustains the physical and emotional pain of being unable to fully understand or stop the bad guys, and his bandaged nose comically symbolizes that failure.

In addition to allusion as part of its construction of character, *The Good German* uses music to subvert the heroic individualism central to *Casablanca* and Hollywood stardom more generally. Thomas Newman's orchestral score recalls the work of his father Alfred on classic-era films such as *The Battle of Midway* (1942) and *December 7th* (1943) for John Ford, Ernst Lubitsh's *Heaven Can Wait* (1943), Elia Kazan's *Gentleman's Agreement* (1947), and Joseph Mankiewicz's *All About Eve* (1950). In the scenes in which Jake and Lena discuss their past, a solo violin sweetly rises above the orchestra, suggesting the return of their prewar love. Yet dissonance marks the younger Newman's music during other exchanges between the couple, as when she hints at her collaboration with the Gestapo during the war, and in the early stages of the climactic parade scene in which Emil is killed. Although the music of the latter scene soon gives way to the bright, even sound of a march that plays as troops pass before a cheering, waving crowd, the earlier dissonant section of Newman's score signals the murder to come, leaving the march to invoke the uncritical patriotism in cultural representations of World War II, of which *Casablanca* is one example.

Jake Geismer's failed plan to save Lena recalls Richard Dyer's important observation about the utopian quality of most Hollywood films. Dyer explains Hollywood's appeal as its ability to successfully represent what most people want and need (abundance, energy, excitement, relationships, community), and its conservatism as a failure to acknowledge the role of inequalities of social power in complicating their attainment (228). *The Good German* rejects such utopian assumptions, just as Soderbergh's most commercial films, *Erin Brockovich, Traffic,* and *Ocean's Eleven,* conversely offer more optimistic endorsements of the viability of the legal system or the possibility to subvert greed and exploitation if you are smart and creative enough. Maybe their upbeat endings are the price Soderbergh has had to pay for the studio resources that allow him access to large audiences. But, consistent with the variety in his movies, *Full Frontal, Bubble, Solaris, The Good German, Che,* and *The Girlfriend Experience* retain the art-film alienation found in his early work. Even with the enormous success of *Traffic, Erin Brockovich,* and the *Ocean's* films, Soderbergh still makes movies that fit the anti-utopian mindset he described in an interview after the release of *Kafka* in 1991: "By nature I am more pessimistic than optimistic, which is not a typically American attitude" (Kaufman 55).

As Dyer asserts, the problem is not the utopian outcomes themselves but Hollywood's oversimplification of how they can be achieved. Soderbergh's most commercial films retain the complex, character-based stories about social injustice typical of almost all his movies, combined with the pleasure of overcoming inequality found in the just resolutions typical of Hollywood narratives. He therefore moves toward a synthesis of the commercial appeal of Hollywood and the more critical nature of art or independent cinema. This synthesis responds to Dyer's assessment of what utopian cinema lacks and gains impact from the access to audiences that it makes possible.

Cinema of Outsiders: Alienation and Crime

Most of Soderbergh's feature films focus on outsider characters who are alienated either by injustice they have witnessed or experienced or because they have been unsuccessful or unwilling to measure up in a world in which self-worth is determined by wealth and power. Major characters in thirteen of his movies—*Kafka, King of the Hill, The Underneath, Out of Sight, The Limey, Traffic, Ocean's Eleven, Ocean's Twelve, Ocean's Thirteen, Bubble, The Good German, The Girlfriend Experience,* and *The Informant!*—act out against this alienation through crime. These narratives validate or at least explain the criminal actions of their main characters as a form of rebellion to which they are driven by the unjust or unfulfilling situations they face. The title character in *Kafka* bombs the laboratory where Dr. Murnau tortures insurgents who resist the repressive government. In *King of the Hill*, twelve-year-old Aaron resorts to petty theft and avoiding creditors to survive the Depression. For the main characters in *The Underneath*, *Out of Sight*, *The Limey*, and the *Ocean's* series, robbery—or, in the case of several characters in *Traffic*, selling illegal drugs—is preferable to what they view as a straight life of hard work with little to show for it. In *Bubble*, Soderbergh presents in stark, realist terms the workplace exploitation and social isolation that lead Martha (Debbie Doebereiner) to murder a coworker who takes advantage of and insults her. For Lena in *The Good German*, the killings she contributes to seem necessary to survive her victimization as a Jew in Berlin during and just after the Second World War. *The Girlfriend Experience* and *The Informant!* show how the pervasive idea of identity defined by consumption erodes moral choices. While locating Chelsea's story of selling herself to pay for an expensive lifestyle in Manhattan parallels prostitution to the finance industry whose executives she services, placing *The Informant!* in middle America (central Illinois) allows Soderbergh to offer the lavish lifestyle paid for by Mark Whitacre's embezzlement as an example of the moral damange to the larger society if the price fixing practiced by senior Archer Daniels Midland executives is accepted as just the cost of doing business in a competitive global economy. These films about alienated outsiders present two related motivations that Nicole Rafter describes as common in movies about crime: "[E]nvironmental causes, illustrating how criminalistic subcultures or other situational factors can drive people to crime," and/or "aspirations for a better life (more money, more excitement, more opportunity to rise through the class structure) . . . crime over dull conformity" (63–64).

Kafka, *King of the Hill*, *Out of Sight*, *Bubble*, *The Good German*, *The Girlfriend Experience*, and *The Informant!* ask us to understand the criminality of their protagonists as reactions to bad circumstances linked to larger social and economic causes. The appeal of the transgressive protagonists in the other six crime films is based less on sociological grounds than through their resemblance to what Robert Ray calls the "outlaw hero" common to Hollywood movies. The outlaw hero acts unilaterally and often with violence—although Soderbergh qualifies such aggression—to bring about a personal sense of justice, and Ray points out that the various incarnations of the outlaw hero as "adventurer, explorer, gunfighter, wanderer, and loner" place the Hollywood films that employ it within "the American imagination valuing self-determination" (59). In *Solaris* and *The Good German*, Soderbergh asked Clooney, whose career was established playing outlaw heroes, to act contrary to type in the service of more complex characterization. In Soderbergh's films as a whole, the viability of the outlaw hero breaks down when stubborn independence becomes an uncaring selfishness, or because of recourse to violence. One or both of these flaws define the villains in his crime films: the sadistic scientist Dr. Murnau in *Kafka*; the bullying cop and the hard-hearted bellboy in *King of the Hill*; the crooked and murderous armored-car-company owner in *The Underneath*; the power-hungry cold-war congressman in *The Good German*; the rich and self-absorbed businessmen Ripley in *Out of Sight* and Valentine in *The Limey*; the even richer and violently vindictive owners of Las Vegas casinos in the *Ocean's* series; and in *Traffic*, the corrupt general (Tomas Milian) who profits from illegal drugs directly, or the self-perpetuating government officials who use them as a political football. The extreme self-interest and/or violence of these unsympathetic characters encourages us to judge less harshly by comparison the criminal behavior of the protagonists, who use crime to push back against the bigger villains, restraining their own selfish behavior in an attempt to reconnect with someone who cares for them. Michael in *The Underneath*, Wilson in *The Limey*, Danny in *Ocean's Eleven*, Jake in *The Good German*, and Rusty in *Ocean's Twelve*—each are driven by a desire to make up for the pain they have caused that special person. Likewise, Kafka, Aaron in *King of the Hill*, Martha in *Bubble*, and the whole crew of thieves in *Ocean's Thirteen* commit crimes not only to protect themselves but also to defend their connection to an important person in their lives. If excessive self-interest is at the root of the injustice these protagonists face, their concern about someone else demonstrates an ability to contain such selfishness.

Rather than show these criminals as strange and monstrous, so that we are drawn to them out of a perverse curiosity, Soderbergh gives us protagonists who are unassuming and sympathetic. They may be played by movie stars like Jeremy Irons, George Clooney, or Brad Pitt, or speak in the codified slang of a criminal subculture like Terence Stamp's Wilson in *The Limey*, yet we recognize ourselves in their failings as they confront problems without clear solutions, make mistakes in their responses, and feel remorse for bad choices. Michael in *The Underneath* wants another try at a successful relationship with his ex-wife after ruining their marriage with a gambling addiction fueled by his need to escape the suburban monotony of his upbringing. During the prison break early in *Out of Sight*, Jack Foley (Clooney) and Karen Sisco (Jennifer Lopez), lying next to each other in the trunk of a getaway car, discuss the 1967 crime film *Bonnie and Clyde* to hint at his character's motivation: like Bonnie (Faye Dunaway)—who, during a quiet moment in bed with Clyde (Warren Beatty), dreams of a "normal" life they might have had without bank robbery and shootouts with lawmen—Foley seeks connection with Sisco in an attempt to "take a time out" from the revolving door that is his life of bank robbery and prison. Recognizing the difficult circumstances they face—they see crime as their only option yet wish for a better course of action—encourages us to take a compassionate view of these characters. Such an attitude toward crime reflects Soderbergh's debt to the New American Cinema of the late 1960s and 1970s—films like *Bonnie and Clyde* or the Lee Marvin revenge picture *Point Blank* (1967), which he has credited as influencing *The Limey*. By the inevitability of their transgressions and the tolerance with which he presents them to us, Soderbergh asks us to understand and empathize with these criminals. Rafter describes the zeitgeist of the New American Cinema in a way that applies to Soderbergh's crime films: "[N]onconformity became heroic, and criminologists taught us that there are few fundamental differences between deviants and the rest of us" (62).

Critical Violence and *Out of Sight*

> Ripley: It must take a lot of balls to walk into a bank and stick it up with a gun, huh?
> Foley: I don't know. I've never used a gun before in my life.
> Ripley: You're kidding.
> Foley: You'd be surprised what all you can get if you ask for it in the right way.
> —Jailyard conversation in *Out of Sight*

While Soderbergh's films encourage us to identify with outsider protagonists, he also qualifies their endorsement of crime by showing the limitations of the violence that often accompanies it. Violence is neither aestheticized, presented as entertainment, nor shown as effective in Soderbergh's films; in fact, criminal rebellion gets sidetracked once it becomes violent. Kakfa's bomb kills Dr. Murnau and destroys his laboratory, yet, like the other attacks by the insurgents from whom he got the explosive device, the political violence of the title character will only justify further government repression. In *The Underneath*, Michael's involvement in the armed robbery of a bank leaves him severly injured and at the mercy of his accomplices' betrayal. After spending most of their adult lives in prison, Foley in *Out of Sight* and Wilson in *The Limey* have accepted the inevitability of violence in the criminal worlds in which they move. They both attempt to embody Ray's self-righteous outlaw hero, yet Foley's use of a gun gets him shot and sent back to prison, and Wilson's plan of violent revenge for the death of his daughter brings him less satisfaction than painful realization of his own failure as a father. Most tragically of all, in *Bubble*, Martha's violent release of the pent-up anger from a lifetime of low-wage work and thankless generosity to others results in the likelihood of a long prison term.

Besides his use of remakes as aesthetic as well as economic opportunities, and the casting of stars in roles that subordinate them to characters and even redefine their images, such critical representation of violence is another way in which Soderbergh has deconstructed the assumptions of Hollywood moviemaking. Central to the spectacle that dominates American film today is graphic violence, which Stephen Prince calls "an inescapable and ubiquitous characteristic of contemporary cinema," despite "a general consensus among social scientists" about its "aggression-inducing characteristics" (*Screening*, 1, 40). Contrary to this status quo in American movies, even in his five heist stories (*The Underneath, Out of Sight,* and *Ocean's Eleven, Twelve,* and *Thirteen*), the two films he has made that involve illegal drugs (*The Limey* and *Traffic*), or *Che*, about revolution—movies whose subject matter creates the expectation of violence—Soderbergh doesn't show much. This becomes apparent when comparing his films to recent movies on similar topics, such as Quentin Tarantino's *Reservoir Dogs* (1992), *Pulp Fiction* (1994), and *Kill Bill: Volumes 1 and 2* (2003, 2004); Michael Mann's *Heat* (1995), *Collateral* (2004), and *Miami Vice* (2007); or a film about insurgents such as Philip Noyce's *The Quiet American* (2002).

What violence the stories in his films make inevitable Soderbergh deglamorizes and deaestheticizes: by portraying it as the only viable response to the Batista government's brutal repression (*Che*); as arising from reluctant acts of self-defense (Michael shooting Tommy in *The Underneath*); as ineffectual (Wilson attacking Valentine on the beach in *The Limey*); as self-destructive (the home invasion near the end of *Out of Sight*); by giving us a distanced, critical view of its brutality (the desert and bomb executions in *Traffic*); by linking it with emotional suffering (Michael's mother mourning Ed's shooting in *The Underneath* or Glen's reaction to the drug-house killings in *Out of Sight*); or by pushing violent conflict offscreen and representing it through sound (the warehouse shootings in *The Limey*). In *Bubble*, the killing is never shown. All we see in the movie's final scene is Martha in jail remembering herself standing over the body of Rose (Misty Wilkins), whom she has just strangled.

Of the thirteen films about crime that Soderbergh has made, the biggest commercial success, *Ocean's Eleven,* contains the most critical portrayal of violence. One example of this critical representation is a montage flashback that Reuben Tishkoff narrates as he tries to dissuade Danny Ocean and Rusty Ryan from their robbery plan by warning them of the greed and ruthlessness of the casino owners. Reuben describes the three most "successful" attempts to steal from a casino on the Strip, all of which end violently for the robber: the first shows the perpetrator tackled; in the second, a security guard flattens him with a nightstick; and in the third, the thief is shot in the back as he runs out of Caesar's Palace with an armful of cash. None of this violence is gracefully aesthetic, spectacularly bloody, nor exciting by virtue of creating heroic empowerment. In fact, Reuben's sarcastic tone emphasizes the stupidity of the attempts that made such violence justifiable; he describes the first robber as a "pencil neck," the second as a "goddam hippy," and the third with: "He came, he grabbed, they conquered." Reuben makes clear that the violence in these robbery attempts represents the determination of the casinos to hold onto their money, and in response to Ocean's and Ryan's plan to rob Tishkoff's arch enemy, Terry Benedict, he warns them: "He better not know you're involved, your names, or think you're dead because he'll kill ya, and then he'll go to work on ya."

The association of the casinos with physical retribution supports the film's larger critique of blockbuster entertainment, Soderbergh's avoidance of violent action in favor of a well-told story about the politics of class. While the conversation with Reuben characterizes the greed of those who run the casinos in terms of their inclination to use violence to protect their profits, Soderbergh is confident of his ability to win over the audience without it. In his DVD commentary, he remarks to the screenwriter Ted Griffin: "I'm not a big fan of shooting guns." Even as the robbery unfolds in *Ocean's Eleven*, Soderbergh leaves violence out, including only a brief scene of the robbers masquerading as a SWAT team to gain entry to the casino vault and firing blanks from their automatic weapons, and another of Danny Ocean pretending to be beaten up. Such fake violence becomes part of the "performance" that is central to the success of the robbery. As the heist itself makes reference to an independent aesthetic—a "crew" of performers and technical experts use skillful acting and storytelling to create a narrative that undermines an enormous entertainment corporation—these examples of staged violence say more about what audiences have learned to expect in crime films than what *Ocean's Eleven* delivers. To underscore how Ocean's crew and Benedict represent not only robbers and their mark but also different ideas of entertainment relative to violence, Benedict attends a prizefight as the nonviolent heist gets off to a successful start.

The distinctiveness of Soderbergh's critical and socially contextualized portrayal of violence becomes clearer when compared to the dominant patterns of how such antisocial behavior is usually represented in American movies. Roger Ebert, long critical of the high level of violence in Hollywood film, has accurately commented that "[t]he movies and television could not exist without relying on stories about people killing each other" (738). Prince points to several explanations for the dramatic increase in explicit movie violence beginning in the 1960s: innovations in the techniques used to represent it (slow motion, squibs, and digitally generated imagery and sound); greater audience interest in films that reflect the violent world to which more viewers had gained more access through television coverage of the Vietnam War and the political assassinations of that period; and relaxed restriction by Hollywood in response to such viewer demand with its adoption of a rating system that made room for violent films produced for mature viewers (*Screening*, 1–13).

Rafter speculates that the prevalence of crime and violence in American movies is motivated by how they give viewers voyeuristic "access to places few of us visit in person"—without the danger of actually going there (11). Because as spectators we aren't really in such dangerous fictional spaces, we can enjoy the excitement of social disorder yet also feel reassured and protected when ultimately, as is often the case in American movies, "justified" violence—often at the hand of an outlaw hero—is used to punish crime and enforce the law.

Soderbergh's crime films avoid these tendencies of American cinema to offer dangerous, disorderly worlds experienced as voyeuristic entertainment and violence as the tool of heroes who reimpose justice. Rather than aggrandize heroes who endorse an ideology of self-reliance, Soderbergh's movies ask us to regard critically characters who attempt to empower themselves through violence. These movies demonstrate the greater effectiveness of intelligence, creativity, and language as responses to injustice, in contrast to the self-imposed disadvantage of those who attempt to live up to the ideal of violent self-determination that Hollywood celebrates. Although not a crime film, *Che* typifies Soderbergh's attitude toward violence as an ineffective technique in fighting injustice. Despite its emphasis on the title character's sense of his mission as a guerilla fighter, the second part of the film, about his failed campaign in Bolivia, makes clear that Guevara's insistence on exporting violent revolution caused his early death and limited his impact on behalf of social change. Soderbergh's interpretation of Che's historical importance therefore emphasizes his service to others rather than his role as a military leader. We see less of Che shooting his weapon than strategizing about how to subvert oppression, or inspiring his colleagues with comments about—or actions that exemplify—an ethos of self-sacrifice and aid to the disadvantaged.

As an example of how crime represents a response to social inequality that can be short-circuited by violence, consider *Out of Sight*. Soderbergh's seventh film, but his first with a big budget (forty-seven million dollars), was made at a low point in his career, when he needed to show that he could return to the level of audience appeal demonstrated by *Sex, Lies, and Videotape* or risk not having the chance to direct at all. Commercial expectations were also generated by the fact that *Out of Sight* is based on a novel by Elmore Leonard, whose work had been successfully translated to the screen by Barry Levinson with his 1995 film *Get Shorty*. *Get Shorty* and *Out of Sight* are both set in criminal worlds made dangerous by African American gangsters (played by Delroy Lindo and Don Cheadle, respectively) whose malicious self-interest is set up to justify the violent justice of white outlaw heroes (John Travolta and Clooney, respectively). In *Out of Sight,* however, these shopworn assumptions about who is in charge and how get short-circuited in favor of a new kind of hero armed with a more strategic approach.

While, typical of Hollywood movies, *Out of Sight* makes upper- and working-class characters a problem and middle class the favored identity, it also shows how economic status contributes to crime and violence (Lehman and Luhr 320). These class values are set up early in the film, when Federal Marshall Karen Sisco is introduced as a hardworking professional with a loving and supportive father who counsels her on her career and buys her Dior suits and an expensive Sig Sauer handgun, while her working-class counterpart, Jack Foley, has spent most of his adult life in what he calls "correctional living" since being introduced to bank robbery at the age of eighteen by an uncle who later died in a charity hospital after serving a long sentence. Sisco "meets" Foley during his escape from prison, when he forces her into the trunk of a getaway car driven by his friend, Buddy (Ving Rhames). Once she is in the trunk, Foley inspects Sisco admiringly with a flashlight and compliments her clothes and perfume, while she complains that the muck that he wears from crawling through a tunnel under the prison fence has ruined the expensive suit her father gave her. When the class difference between Jack and Karen is set aside briefly later in the film—long enough for them to spend the night together in a Detroit hotel—it requires that Foley pretend to adopt her middle-class status by buying new clothes and shoes appropriate for the occasion.

The contrasting class status of Sisco and Foley is reflected in their different attitudes toward work. The feminist dimension of *Out of Sight,* whereby Karen shows her competence to her father and the male FBI supervisior who doubt her, builds upon the character's confident middle-class assumption about her ability to prove herself through her job. Conversely, Foley operates with less optimism that his work will be rewarded. He commits two crimes in *Out of Sight*: a failed bank robbery that lands him back in prison, and the invasion of the suburban Detroit home of the financier Richard Ripley (Albert Brooks) in search of five million dollars in uncut diamonds. Both crimes are directly motivated by a flashback scene in which Jack goes to Ripley for the job he was promised when the two men were in prison together, only to have his distrust of work confirmed. Ripley offers Foley a job as a security guard in his office building. Acknowledging that it is a "lousy job with a lousy wage," Ripley insists that because of Foley's criminal background as a bank robber, he must prove himself: "You're a bank robber. It's not a very marketable skill. You have to earn something better." Foley's angry response is the most direct statement of *Out of Sight*'s take on class in American society: Ripley hasn't "earn[ed] something better" but rather understands how to use deception to establish his economic interests. Ripley's rationalization for underpaying those who work for him demonstrates that understanding, while Foley's angry response to the job offer—legitimate though it may be—keeps him in a disadvantaged position: "Don't give me that Knute Rockne pull-yourself-up-by-your-bootstraps bullshit. You married a rich broad with a company, sold it off in pieces, and divorced her. When we were in prison, you were ice cream for freaks. Snoopy Miller and a dozen other guys would have bled you until you were less than nothing. I protected you." After these angry words, Foley turns down the job. A shot omitted from the final cut but included in the DVD's extra features shows him breaking a fish tank in Ripley's office with a paperweight, incensed that the position's lack of responsibility and remuneration don't acknowledge the dangerous work he has already done to protect Ripley, but also because it would simply replicate his life in prison, watching the investor's back. As in *The Underneath, The Limey, Traffic,* and *Ocean's Eleven,* when Soderbergh shows how working-class men find themselves in jobs that put them in danger, challenging the status quo means confronting other men from a similar social background who have agreed to do its dirty work. In *Out of Sight,* this lack of choice is manifested by the two security guards who throw Foley out of Ripley's office after he turns down the job they already occupy.

Foley's comment to Ripley and his subsequent violent outburst also recall the confrontation earlier in the film that shows him protecting the financier from the attempt by Maurice "Snoopy" Miller (Don Cheadle) to shake him down while the three are in prison. In that scene, Miller describes his power within the prison population based on physical force using the language of stocks and investment, as if to (mistakenly) parallel that violent authority with Ripley's economic privilege in the outside world. Foley's angry reaction to the "lousy job with a lousy wage" replicates this mistaken overvaluation of anger and violence. As *Out of Sight* clearly shows, unsanctioned violence used by working-class men often results in incarceration and/or physical harm to them. As a former boxer who washed out of the fight game in favor of selling illegal drugs and home invasions and winds up dead by the movie's conclusion, Miller exemplifies both of these outcomes.

While the working-class criminals in *Out of Sight* exaggerate the value of their skills with violence and, like Ripley, concern themselves too much with the quick money that they pursue through illegal actions, Karen Sisco's professionalism demonstrates the greater value of meaningful work. The sociologist Alberto Arenas defines four motivations for work: to provide for basic needs, to gain a higher standard of living and greater social prestige, to feel satisfaction from work done well, and to acquire moral value from improving one's community and/ or environment. While none of the criminals in *Out of Sight*, including Ripley, get beyond the first two motivations, Sisco's success in law enforcement brings her the greater satisfaction of all four. We see Foley's self-confidence and charisma in the opening scene, when he robs a Miami bank, but his quick arrest reminds us that such "work" has no currency in the straight world. In contrast, Sisco consistently overcomes the gender bias of her father and her mostly male law-enforcement collegues and demonstrates her excellence on the job by finding Foley and stopping the home invasion in Ripley's suburban mansion. While bringing in working-class criminals and protecting Ripley may appear to reinforce the patriarchal status quo, unlike Foley or Miller and his colleagues, Sisco doesn't directly contribute to her own subjugation, and her successes undercut the limits on women's opportunities imposed by the male characters' conservative ideas of gender.

This feminist dimension to Sisco's character also contributes to *Out of Sight's* revision of film-noir conventions. Several aspects of the film characterize it as a noir: its investigative narrative set in worlds of crime and violence; its low-key visual style in the latter half of the movie, once the story moves to Detroit; and especially a logic of obsessive desire manifested in the romance between the federal marshall and the criminal. Yet, despite such fidelity to generic conventions, Sisco's appropriation of the investigator role and the resulting reversal of the film's male star into an *homme fatale* present not only a revised picture of gender in noir but also a new version of the outlaw hero. Typical of the outlaw hero, Sisco solves a breach in justice by going on her own to track down Foley and the other thieves he gets involved with. Yet, as both an agent of law enforcement and a character who plays by her own rules—particulary as she pursues her own sexual as well as career goals with Foley—Sisco reconciles the contradictory values of responsibility to others inherent in her job with the individualism of her desire. As Linda Mizejewski puts it in her analysis of *Out of Sight*, the film "allows her to succeed with the case and have the outlaw lover too" (156). Such a reconciliation of Sisco's forceful individualism and the collective good maximizes her appeal to viewers who believe in both sets of values.

Because this reconciliation of self-interest with concern about others is enacted by one character, usually the film's star, Ray regards it as inherently favoring an ideology of individualism. Yet in *Out of Sight*, not only does Sisco reconcile her own desire with the traditional feminine ideal concern for others, she also balances middle-class ideas of career with noir's challenge to economic privilege. As Peter Lehman and William Luhr point out, "Film noir may be seen in linked class and gender terms. Many of its films . . . involve women who aspire above their 'place' in both gender and class. Neither submissive nor maternal, they exploit their sexuality to manipulate and often destroy men in their ruthless attempts to rise in class" (327). By making the Lopez character both an investigator representing the law and transgressive, *Out of Sight* reinforces the status quo (as she advances her career and stops criminals) but also undercuts it (by undermining male bias against her and at the same time satisfying her desire for Foley). In the final scene, as she transports Foley back to the Glades Prison in Florida from which he escaped, we learn that she has delayed the trip so he could ride with another convict who has escaped from prison nine times. She is doing her job with the usual efficiency, yet the implication is that Karen also wants Foley to learn how to escape again. Combined with the fact that Buddy has gotten away with millions in uncut diamonds taken from Ripley, we assume that, once out, he would succeed in staying free—and available to Karen. Although before the Ripley robbery we hear Foley ask Buddy with a tone of doubt, "Do you know anyone who's done one big score and gone on to live the good life?" the conclusion of *Out of Sight* implies just such a criminal subversion of the hierarchy of class, facilitated by Karen Sisco's ability to appear to support while undercutting the patriarchal legal system. Furthermore, just as Sisco's revised outlaw hero limits her use of violence to two instances of self-defense, the successful robbery of the diamonds involves Foley and Buddy taking them from a second fish tank in Ripley's home, this one unbroken by angry aggression.

Chris Holmlund has summed up Sisco's tightrope walk as "post-feminist," whereby she "gets it all"—the advantages for women made possible by feminism, along with the approval of men brought about by a conventionally feminine appearance (118). This is certainly true, but it is important to recognize how Sisco similarly balances career success with a subversion of a male-controlled system justified by the promise of reward for work. Another way to state this point would be in terms of Arenas's hierarchy of motiviations for work. Sisco achieves the most meaningful work by earning a living, moving up as a result of her success on the job, feeling the fulfillment of doing her job well and the moral satisfaction of subverting unfair ideas of gender that deny opportunities to women and the hypocrisy of a society that claims to promote individual freedom and achievement but in fact protects the privilege of those few with wealth like Ripley.

This critique of class privilege in *Out of Sight* goes beyond recycling the Hollywood populist convention of favoring the hard-working middle-class or the upwardly mobile working-class character over the arrogant and pampered rich by invoking political and economic changes in American society during the 1980s and 1990s that contributed to crime, and the accompanying ideas that gained currency about its causes and how to control it. David Garland summarizes the effects of the political conservatism of that period as resulting in a less "solidaristic" and more "exclusionary" culture, committed to social control rather than provision for those most in need. Private freedoms supportive of market growth therefore took precedence over "the public freedoms of . . . citizenship" (193).

The deindustrialization, downsizing, and outsourcing of jobs during those two decades created what Garland calls "an increasingly insecure economy" that marginalized "substantial sections of the population" of the United States, while simultaneously putting greater emphasis on consumption. In a report on the growth of consumer spending since 1980, the economist Mitra Toossi in 2002 summarized that "[c]onsumer demand is the main force behind the U.S. economy" (20). An increasing gulf between haves and have-nots, pressure to consume, and what Garland calls "low levels of . . . community solidarity" together resulted in a crime-conscious culture in the 1980s and 1990s, eager to "segregate, fortify, and exclude" (194). Steven D. Levitt concludes that two of the main reasons for the decline in crime in the United States during the 1990s were increased rates of incarceration and more police, both evidence of such greater interest in security and separation of the haves from the have-nots (164).

Garland notes that this trend toward more incarceration and protection of private space was largely "directed against those groups most adversely affected by the dynamics of economic and social change—the urban poor . . . minority communities" and was based on an assumption of responsibility lying with those who commit crime, what Garland calls "the themes that dominate crime policy—rational choice and the structures of control" (196). However, this emphasis on personal responsibility was not extended to the upper-income levels of American society, resulting in "more controls . . . imposed on the poor, while fewer and fewer controls affect the market freedoms of the rest" (197).

In addition to gender and class inequality, incarceration and social segregation are central issues in *Out of Sight*'s portrayal of crime. Most of the movie's first thirty minutes show Foley in or breaking out of prison. After his escape, he tells Sisco that he has spent half his life in jail and would do another thirty years if caught. Once the story shifts from Florida to Detroit, Foley, Buddy, and several other former inmate accomplices go after the diamonds that Ripley carelessly told them about when they were locked up together in California. Although Ripley's fraud convictions were serious enough to warrant a fifteen-million-dollar fine (that he paid with a check), his three-year sentence, short in comparison to the time Foley faces, demonstrates Garland's point that American law punishes the transgressions more likely to be committed by the poor than those related to perversions of "market freedoms."

Moving the story to Detroit, the setting for much of Leonard's crime fiction, allows *Out of Sight* to emphasize the class and racial issues that impact crime and the American legal system's response to it. As Ted Mouw points out, the loss of industrial jobs from Detroit after 1970 disproportionately impacted the city's large African American population; in 1990, black unemployment in the Motor City was more than three times that of whites (736). Foley's plan involves him with African American thieves, most notably Buddy and "Snoopy" Miller, and the credibility of Clooney's character is bolstered by his ability to adopt the "cool" confidence associated with African American masculinity. In his analysis of race in *Out of Sight,* Todd Boyd comments that Foley "holds his own in a world otherwise dominated by Black men" (119). In support of this racial dimension of Clooney's character, Soderbergh changed the Buddy character from the white former auto worker of Leonard's novel to an African American played by Ving Rhames. Foley's cool confidence as the crime unfolds comes from his nothing-to-lose attitude shared by Buddy and Cheadle's "Snoopy" Miller, an indifference created by the three men's experience of disadvantage as an incentive for criminal careers and brought into relief by their hostile antagonism toward Ripley's wealth.

In the scene in which Ripley offers a job to Foley, the financier articulates the assumption of individual responsibility that Garland describes as dominant in the discourse on crime in 1980s and 1990s America. Ripley justifies the low-wage security-guard position he offers Foley as necessary to provide the ex–bank robber a chance to prove he has given up his criminal past. Yet the security in Ripley's office building and his residence in a remote suburb create what Garland calls an "iron cage" in which he is confined by his vulnerability and dependent on others for protection (204). Karen Sisco stops the home invasion and apprehends Jack, yet the story nonetheless supports property crime as a valid response to class inequality, as Buddy slips away with the uncut diamonds into the snowy night—a wintry and dark setting that offers a visual metaphor for the racial conflict within the story, and a successful robbery that sums up how Soderbergh sneaks a social critique of crime and the legal system into *Out of Sight* under the cover of star performances and noir obsessions.

Words as Weapons: *The Limey* and *Ocean's Eleven*

Like *Out of Sight, The Limey* questions the efficacy of violence to address class inequality, and in its place language is foregrounded as an effective means with which to negotiate social position. On one level, *The*

Limey offers a genre story about a father, Wilson (Terence Stamp), looking for revenge for the death of his daughter, Jenny (Melissa George). However, the allusive use of footage from Ken Loach's 1967 film *Poor Cow*, showing Stamp as a young criminal arrested and sent to jail, and the narration that moves back and forth in time to demonstrate the controlling power of memory allow Soderbergh to privilege character over plot and insert authorial statement in a manner characteristic of the art film. The movie's genre tendencies fit the main character's view of the world—Wilson's need for revenge is driven by his belief that violence is necessary to achieve justice—yet it becomes apparent that he seeks vengeance to displace the guilt he feels from spending most of his adult life in prison and therefore not having parented his daughter.

As Wilson pursues the man directly responsible for his daughter's death—her boyfriend, Terry Valentine (Peter Fonda)—we see how alike the two men are, and how they are both pursuing the same conception of personal success founded on the acquisition of money and power over others, even when that requires violence. In contrast to such a pathological notion of self-empowerment, the story defines Jenny, her former acting teacher Elaine (Leslie Ann Warren), and her classmate Eduardo (Luis Guzman) primarily in terms of their concern for others. As a girl, Jenny became alienated from her father and as an adult challenged Valentine because of the impact of the men's criminal actions on her life as well as theirs. Out of loyalty to their dead friend, Elaine and Eduardo help Wilson find out what happened to Jenny, but they disagree with his desire for violent revenge. Such pursuit of revenge, driven by the conception of self-assertion that has governed Wilson for his whole life, in no way resolves the injustice of Jenny's death; it simply replicates the same violent destructiveness.

Language is an important part of the film's critique of unilateral, "justified" violence. As Sarah Kozloff points out, "[W]hat the characters say, exactly how they say it, and how the dialogue is integrated with the rest of the cinematic techniques are crucial to our experience and understanding of every film" (6). Assuming the visual particularity of film, theory and criticism often deemphasizes the linguistic component of movies, emphasizing instead what Noel Carroll calls "the specificity thesis," which "envision[s] each art form on the model of a highly specialized tool with a range of determinate functions. . . . If you wish to explore the potentials of aesthetically crafted language, use theater. If your topic is animated action, use film. . . . But I think it is incumbent on us to question whether this underlying metaphor has any applicability when it comes to art forms. Are art forms highly specialized tools? . . . They can be used to do many things" ("Specificity" 326).

Although Soderbergh pays careful attention to visual style, language is an equally important part of his movies. Words function in his films to articulate the grievances of outsider protagonists, but also as a more effective way for them to negotiate their social interactions and conflicts than the violence that Hollywood so often prefers. While it may be true, as Stephen Prince states, that the kinetic nature of cinema makes it an effective medium for representing violence, the verbal dimension of cinematic storytelling offers a way for Soderbergh to offset the negative social results of such violence, within his narratives and potentially on the audience. About the impact of film violence on viewers, Prince concludes: "For those concerned about the contemporary state of American visual culture, the present fetish for explicit gore is a worrisome development, given the evidence that now exists . . . about the effects on viewers of repeated exposure to violent images and narratives" (*Savage Cinema* 2).

At numerous points in Soderbergh's crime films, the effective use of language functions to address the social inequities and alienation that create narrative conflict, or, conversely, a lack of verbal communication is shown to contribute to such problems. In *The Limey*, Wilson's manner of speaking tells us about his cultural and class origins but also creates miscommunication with other characters that leads to violence. When he investigates his daughter's death at a downtown warehouse, his use of Cockney rhyming slang (whereby the intended word rhymes with the word spoken) annoys the foreman (William Lucking) of a group of men who had helped Valentine transport drugs. Violence quickly follows the failure of language, and Wilson shoots several of the men, alerting Valentine to the fact that he is after him. A similar scene of language failure and recourse to violence occurs when Wilson is taken into custody and questioned by a DEA agent (Bill Duke). In the course of his revenge plan, he has stumbled into the agency's investigation of Valentine:

WILSON: How ya doin there, all right are ya? Now, look squire, you're the governor here, I can see that I'm on your manor now. So, no need to get your knickers in a twist. Whatever the bollocks is goin' down between you and that slag Valentine, it's got nothing to do with me. . . . Let me explain. When I was in prison—second time, no, third. Third stretch, yeah. There was this screw that really had it in for me. That geezer was top of my list. Two years after I got sprung, I saw him in Arnold Park. He was sitting on a bench feeding bloody pidgeons. There was no one else about. I coulda gone up behind him and snapped his fucking neck. But I left it. Coulda nobbled him, but I didn't. 'Cos what I thought I wanted wasn't what I wanted. What I thought I was thinking about was something else. I didn't give a toss . . . 'cos you got to make a choice . . . and you can act accordingly.

DEA AGENT: There's one thing I don't understand. The thing I don't understand . . . is every motherfucking word you're saying.

By claiming not to understand Wilson, the agent dismisses his anecdote about choosing to avoid violence and, once they agree on their common interest in stopping Valentine, lets slip information as to where he can be found. With the stage set for Wilson's revenge to proceed, the interview concludes with a validation of that course of action:

DEA AGENT: See, crooks move faster than the system, so if we're going to clean up the neighborhood, we don't have time to wait for things like search warrants and trials. Procedure becomes what you got to do . . .
WILSON: Cheers, mate.
DEA AGENT: Go with God.

Wilson's colloquial language, like his rhyming slang that led to the conflict in the warehouse scene, makes it difficult for the agent to understand him, and the characters use such miscommunication to choose a violent, vigilante reaction to Valentine's criminal actions rather than a discursive response involving warrants, evidence, and a trial. The DEA agent's statement about the need to act without recourse to the legal system was added to Lem Dobbs's original script, and Soderbergh shoots the dialogue with a series of jump cuts, offering us a distanced position from which to think critically about the version of justice they agree upon. Moreover, consistent with Soderbergh's inclination toward allusion, Duke's presence evokes a 1993 film, *Deep Cover*, that he directed about another DEA agent (Charles Martin Smith) who recruits a cop

(Laurence Fishburne) to infiltrate a drug cartel and do whatever is necessary, including violence and drug dealing, to bring down its leaders. Fishburne's character finally gives up on this plan, realizing that what he's doing isn't reducing the damage that drugs do to African American communities like the one he grew up in but instead supports the interest of government officials and the heads of the drug business. In *The Limey*, Wilson's vigilante violence, sanctioned by the DEA, proves equally unproductive.

Oddly enough, in contrast to the failure of language in a character-centered independent film like *The Limey*, one of the best examples in Soderbergh's movies of language working more effectively than violence is *Ocean's Eleven*, where the big budget could have allowed for lots of action if he had chosen to show it. In the following comment, however, Soderbergh refers to his choice of how to do the film: "When I say *Ocean's Eleven* is a throwback to an earlier period in cinema, I mean that the movie is never mean, it's never gratuitous, nobody is killed, nobody is humiliated for no reason or is the butt of a joke. . . . I didn't think darker or meaner ideas had a place. . . . I wanted it to be sparkling" (Cheshire 2). For Danny Ocean and his eleven accomplices to successfully rob three Las Vegas casinos of $150 million without any violence requires that they rely heavily on the power of language to deceive. If Sarah Kozloff is correct that "as the gangster is unrestrained in his approach to violence, so is he promiscuous in his approach to words," conversely Ocean and his disciplined crooks make every word count (212). The only members of the crew who talk too much are the argumentative brothers (Scott Caan and Casey Affleck), and when it comes to work, even their verbal sparring functions to distract casino security. As Kozloff explains, the gangster talks a lot as a means of intimidation—to create the kind of humiliation and to complement the violence that Soderbergh wanted to avoid. Instead, Ocean and his number two, Rusty Ryan, use the economy of their speech to create curiosity and to persuade in ways that make the heist successful.

To demonstrate this use of dialogue to create curiosity and confidence in support of the heist, the following analysis will briefly examine several scenes from *Ocean's Eleven*. All of them emphasize what Ocean and Ryan say as the organizers of the robbery. Not only do they use words to influence other characters within the narrative, their dialogue also stokes the audience's interest in, and confidence about, how the heist will play out.

In its first scene, *Ocean's Eleven* sets up curiosity and persuasion as important tools of its title character and the story itself. The film opens with Ocean appearing before a parole board charged with deciding whether he should leave prison after serving five years on a robbery conviction. As he answers the board's questions, Ocean is polite, succinct, and direct in an effort to convince those in control of his freedom that his crime was motivated purely by the emotional distress of his marriage ending and that he is resolute about staying on the straight and narrow from then on:

> UNSEEN PAROLE BOARD MEMBER: Was there a reason you chose to commit this crime?
> OCEAN: My wife left me. I was upset. I got into a self-destructive pattern.
> SECOND UNSEEN PAROLE BOARD MEMBER: Is it likely you'd fall back into a similar pattern?
> OCEAN: She already left me once. I don't think she'll do it again just for kicks.

The viewer who is aware that this is a story about a heist, or that Clooney has previously played charming criminals in films such as *Out of Sight* and *Three Kings,* should doubt the truth of Ocean's answers and wonder what he is really up to. Yet the simplicity and directness of his responses allow for the possibility that they persuade their diegetic listeners. The gap between the parole board's acceptance of the truth of his answers and our doubt is pointed to by the conclusion of the scene. One of the board members asks Ocean, "What do you think you would do if released?" The shot ends before he answers, suggesting that whatever he tells them will be a lie to get out of prison, and the real answer to the board member's question will be the rest of the movie to come.

The power of language to generate curiosity and facilitate persuasion are again laid out as a main theme in the scene soon afterward in which Ocean meets up with Ryan in Los Angeles. Words functioning in these two ways are connected with gambling as a preview of what the story has in store for us. Together, the two men take thousands of dollars from a group of naïve young television actors whom Pitt's character is ostensibly teaching to play poker. When asked what he does for a living, Ocean reveals that he "steals things" and is just out of prison, making the young actors wary and curious about the mysterious figure in their game and distracting them so that Ryan can orchestrate the take by building up the idea that Ocean is bluffing with a weak hand.

In the subsequent scenes in which Ocean and Ryan plan the job and put together the crew, we learn very little about how the heist will work, other than it is highly ambitious and seemingly impossible because of the extensive security at the casinos. The lack of description from Ocean and Ryan, combined with the seemingly long odds, only makes us more curious about the job itself. The economy of their speech as they explain the heist to their collaborators not only heightens the mystery about it but also allows the personal motivations of the other thieves to persuade them to join.

In the case of two important participants—Reuben, the financier of the job, and Saul (Carl Reiner), the confidence man who will get them access to the casinos's safe—Ryan and Ocean overcome their initial skepticism by flattering the vanity of the older men, complimenting their accomplishments and critical acumen about the business of robbery. Yet they also persuade them by sparking Reuben's desire to get even with Terry Benedict and Saul's to return to the game and escape the boredom of retirement.

Perhaps the most persuasive scenes in which *Ocean's Eleven* establishes the dominance of language over violence are those in which Benedict speaks to Ryan and Ocean immediately after the money has been taken. Benedict's inclination to use violence to get what he wants is hinted at earlier in the film, when Reuben comments that "he [Benedict] muscled me out" of the casino business, and then after the robbery, when Reuben threatens Ryan over the phone: "When I find you, I won't call the police. I'll take care of it myself." This threat of violence reveals Benedict's weakness with language, which soon comes back to haunt him. In the subsequent scene, Ocean gets Benedict to agree to give up his relationship with Tess if they return the stolen money, while, unbeknownst to the casino owner, she watches and listens via a closed-circuit television hookup. Again, Ocean's language persuades Benedict that this exchange is possible and Tess that, although he may be a liar and a thief, such an elaborate and dangerous verbal game also proves that he loves her, while Benedict clearly prefers the money. Soderbergh's use of dialogue to establish the main characters' motives and at the same time arouse the curiosity and identification of the audience may sound like nothing new. Generating curiosity and expectation about narrative events and establishing identification with main characters have long been central to the Hollywood mode of storytelling. However, Soderbergh's interest in such a "throwback" type of filmmaking offers an alternative to the contemporary predominance of adolescent comedies and action blockbusters in which exaggerated caricature, violent, digitally enhanced spectacle, and marketing have displaced well-constructed characters and narratives. Such allusion to Hollywood's kinder, gentler past allows Soderbergh access to a larger audience for the social commentary associated with his version of independent cinema.

Independent Form

While Geoff King agrees that American independent cinema has always been a relational designation and therefore "not entirely separable from Hollywood," he nonetheless presents three distinguishing characteristics: "lower budgets and less marketing-driven filmmaking," to increase creative control; "challenging perspectives on social issues, a rarity in Hollywood"; and disruption of "the smoothly flowing conventions associated with mainstream Hollywood style" (1–2).

Almost all of Soderbergh's films fit into one or more of King's criteria for independent cinema. Small budgets and aesthetic choices winning out over market considerations certainly describe his first six films, as well as more recent movies like *Full Frontal, Bubble,* and *The Girlfriend Experience.* As his budgets have grown, Soderbergh has retained a large measure of creative control, as demonstrated by the use of stars in roles that subordinate their images to characters and by how, even in high-profile films like *Erin Brockovich, Traffic,* and two of the three *Ocean's* films, he hasn't shied away from stories that critique greed and link crime to inequality. His control has also been demonstrated by fairly expensive recent movies like *Solaris, The Good German,* and *Che,* which had limited commercial potential because of their subversion of genre or strong political positions.

But just as his movies respond to social injustice both by representing its cost in alienated protagonists as well as with outsider heroes who succeed in fighting back, likewise Soderbergh's formal style is varied, fitting together incongruent tendencies: the objective realism and stylization to express character psychology that coexist in the art film, but also a contemporary version of the continuity form typical of Hollywood linear narrative. Soderbergh refers to this hybrid approach when he talks about "'infusing American material with a European film aesthetic,'" so that, with the help of genre stories—a biopic in *Kafka,* a kidpic in *King of the Hill,* noir in *The Underneath, Out of Sight,* and *The Good German,* the revenge story in *The Limey,* the social-problem film in *Erin Brockovich, Traffic,* and *The Informant!* and the heist picture for the *Ocean's* series—"you can play on two levels. The audience is there to see a film of a certain type, . . . meanwhile you can indulge in some of your personal preoccupations without it becoming too pretentious or boring'" (qtd. in Biskind 191).

To illustrate how this synthesis of art-film realism and stylization with Hollywood continuity works, allow me to start with David Bordwell's descriptions of both types of form. According to Bordwell, three procedural schemata structure the plot and style of the art film: "'objective realism,' 'expressive' or subjective realism, and narrational commentary" ("Art-Cinema Narration" 205). Location shooting, use of available light, and handheld camera—most pronounced in *Traffic, Bubble, Full Frontal, Che,* and *The Girlfriend Experience* but present also to some degree in *Erin Brockovich, Out of Sight, The Limey,* and even the *Ocean's* films—demonstrate Soderbergh's inclination toward objective realism. The veteran gaffer James Planette offered the following description of *Ocean's Eleven:* "'The lighting was very reality-based. First we looked at what the reality was, and then we tried to make it work. We may have needed to enhance a few things for dramatic purposes or just to get an exposure, but we wanted the movie to look as if it wasn't lit at all'" (qtd. in Bankston). Soderbergh has described such objective realism as an important way to engage audiences: "[T]he more real it feels and the less it feels like a Hollywood movie, the more audiences will connect with it" (Smith 29).

Bordwell points to "abrupt cutting" and long takes as "flexible" formal devices that can communicate either objective realism or character subjectivity, depending on the context ("Art-Cinema Narration" 206). Soderbergh takes advantage of such flexibility to use a long take in the interrogation scene of *Bubble* to give us a good look at the distress registered on Martha's face as Detective Don Taylor (Dexter Moody) presents her with the evidence of her guilt. Conversely, another long take done with a handheld camera in *Ocean's Eleven,* as Brad Pitt and Topher Grace enter a Los Angeles nightclub, preserves continuous space and time that would have suited Bazin. In a shootout scene between DEA agents, the San Diego Police, and drug smugglers in *Traffic,* quick cutting conveys the confusion of the violence and lack of coordination between law-enforcement agencies. Rapid cutting also helps Soderbergh represent subjective realism in several of his films, as with the discontinuity editing used to show a rapid play of thought and memory in *The Underneath, The Limey,* or *Out of Sight.* While Hollywood may present characters with clear and unified traits and goals that would be viewed from an objective standpoint as "real," the art film instead frequently offers subjectivity, marked by alienation and ambivalence communicated through formal disjunction, as more lifelike (Bordwell, "Art-Cinema Narration," 206). As we have seen, Soderbergh's love for outsider protagonists explains his inclination toward the latter type of expressive realism. While the invisible form of Hollywood defines characters mainly through their words and actions, expressive realism often uses stylized mise-en-scène, camerawork, editing, sound, music, light, color, and narrative overtness— flashbacks and even flash forwards—to communicate character traits or to present authorial commentary. By using both objectively realist and stylized formal patterns, Soderbergh's films therefore function "beneath" and "beyond" Hollywood's continuity, at times using the conventions of documentary to present a lower level of artifice and more authenticity, and at other moments stylizing beyond the norm of Hollywood's invisible form (King, *American Independent,* 107).

To the degree that Soderbergh's films contain an element of Hollywood continuity form, they follow what Bordwell calls the dominant visual style in American cinema during the last forty years: "intensified continuity . . . traditional continuity amped up, raised to a higher pitch of emphasis" (*Way Hollywood* 120). One characteristic of this intensified continuity is rapid editing—in shot/reverse shot conversations as much as in blockbuster action sequences—that allows for fewer establishing shots but therefore even greater adherence to the 180-degree rule to keep viewers oriented as shots rush past (124). Bordwell notes that many filmmakers now use long lenses to facilitate shooting on location along with closely framed shots of individual actors, "singles," that "allow the director . . . to pick the best bits of each actor's performance" (130). Such singles have become increasingly common, as opposed to group compositions or the *plan américain* medium-long shot characteristic of Classic Hollywood (130). Besides faster cutting, a variety of lens length, and singles, intensified continuity has made the camera more mobile, as push-ins, circling or crane shots, and/or handheld shooting have become more common, bringing energy and volume to the image. Bordwell sums up these four characteristics: "A fast cutting rate, the bipolar extremes of lens lengths, a reliance on tight singles, and the free-ranging camera are salient marks of intensified continuity. Virtually every contemporary mainstream American film will exhibit at least some of them" (137).

To explain the development of this intensified continuity, Bordwell points to several causes, including the cost pressures of faster and more location shooting and the video and digital technology that have become commonplace in feature-film production. But he emphasizes in particular the influence of television, whereby films are generally seen on smaller screens than in theaters and in a distracted environment common to home viewing, prompting filmmakers to try to grab viewer attention with "animated visuals," particularly fast cutting, expressive, tight framing, and dynamic camera movements. Frederick Wasser describes this change in film style in a way that echoes several of the characteristics Bordwell describes and adds digital imagery and multichannel sound as additional elements in the strategy of filmmakers to hold viewer interest: "There are many visual wonders that can play on television, and it is not surprising that today's big-budget movies emphasize these. They can be summarized as those things that give a movie the visceral pleasure of a roller-coaster ride, such as powerful camera moves, morphing and other digital enhancements, and quick editing. . . . The ear has also assumed new importance. Full stereo with surround sound gives a greater dimensional feeling to the film for both the theater audience and to those home viewers who have . . . multiple speakers" (*Veni* 196–97).

Of all Soderbergh's films, the *Ocean's* series comes closest to intensified continuity, with moving master shots, rapid editing, split screens, slow-motion, and montage sequences laid over David Holmes's snappy score to stylize already upbeat narratives. Yet even in these three blockbuster films, such "overtness" is as much about defining character and authorial commentary as generating raw kinetic energy or emotional power to hold viewer attention. Moreover, the realism of actual locations and handheld camera in these three films reminds us of Soderbergh's social engagement and interest in a hybrid aesthetic—created by mixing such verisimilitude with the familiarity of genre and absorbing storytelling. Bordwell comments that art cinema appears to be working at odds when it combines realism and stylization, yet that ambiguity rewards active viewers who make sense of its complexity. Similarly, Soderbergh's use of familiar genre conventions and an emphasis on narrative clarity may reassure viewers, but his addition of realism and stylized characterization also opens up the possibility for critical viewing.

Because of Clooney's presence, Holmes's music, and its world of charismatic thieves and love made dangerous by the business of crime, *Out of Sight* seems like a prequel to the *Ocean's* films. Yet formally the earlier movie turns the dial more toward art-film discontinuity. *Out of Sight* opens with a blurred image of downtown Miami. The camera then tilts up and freezes on the first title, "Universal Pictures Presents," after which the image racks into focus, zooms back, and pans left, only to freeze again on a second title: "A Jersey Films Production." The camera then continues panning until it finds Jack Foley in extreme long shot, exiting an office building, removing his tie and throwing it to the pavement in disgust. The next shot cuts in on Foley and repeats the tie throwing. A wipe-by cut moves us in even closer on Foley's annoyed face, and we watch him look left. An eyeline match then shows us the Sun Trust Bank sign he sees, and the opening scene wraps up with three shots in extreme long shot and medium close-up showing him crossing the street to begin his robbery.

Energized by the catchy Hammond organ lead-in to the Isley Brothers' "It's Your Thing, Do What You Wanna Do," the hyperactive camera movement and cutting of this opening scene engage viewer attention and present Foley's volatile character quickly. At the same time, however, the documentary quality of the location setting, long lens shots, available light, and shaky camerawork imply a larger context for the single of his angry rejection of the tie as a symbol of respectability and authority. Especially in his more realist films—such as *Erin Brockovich, Traffic,* and *Bubble,* but even in stylized stories such as *Out of Sight* and *The Limey*—Soderbergh alternates between objective long shots and closer compositions to show us characters within a larger narrative space and in closer views that specify their alienated reactions to their environment.

The Limey, another film about a career criminal at odds with his world, opens with stylistic similarities to *Out of Sight*'s introduction. The arrival of Wilson at LAX starts with an expressive close-up, showing the character's angry determination, followed by several long shots implying his antagonisms: an eyeline to two cops outside the terminal and several more as he travels to a nearby motel, where we see him contemplate his revenge. As with *Out of Sight,* the opening scene in *The Limey* presents the realistic look of location shooting and available light, and the alienation of its protagonist is established by music as well as visually: the angry working-class rock of the Who, in this case, rather than the Isley Brothers' assertion of independence from the control of Motown mogul Barry Gordy used in the opening of *Out of Sight.*

Throughout its exposition, *The Limey* continues to combine intensified continuity—rapid cutting, singles, and the alternation of long and short focal-length compositions—with art-film realism and character subjectivity communicated through discontinuity editing. After Wilson arrives at his motel, he takes another cab to the home of his daughter's friend, Eduardo, to find out about her death. This scene mixes singles in close and medium close-ups with long shots, and begins—as does the following violent sequence at a warehouse—with a moving master shot typical of a highly kinetic intensified style without time for a more static view of the larger narrative space. Yet as such cinematography conveys Wilson's plans for vindication, following the conventions of the genre by which, as Nicole Rafter puts it, revenge films "spell out the motives of those who take the law into their own hands," Soderbergh and the cinematographer Ed Lachman also subvert our expectations of vigilante justice through discontinuity editing that encourages critical distance by showing the contradictions between Wilson's plans and the connectedness he wants to recover from his past (157). Lachman has explained that the rapid flashbacks and -forwards early in the film are meant to show where Wilson came from and where he is going, specifically his memories of Jenny and the desire for revenge that animate his "interior world" (Williams 56). Lachman, who would go on to use a similar hybrid style as Soderbergh's cinematographer on *Erin Brockovich*, was experienced in such visual representation of character subjectivity, having worked previously with Godard, Herzog, Wenders, and Sven Nykvist. While the first two scenes showing Wilson as he decides upon his plans for violent retribution are made up exclusively of singles, the subsequent scenes, as he begins to pursue his revenge, retain the alternation between long shots and medium close-up or close-up framing but also begin to add compositions that group characters together to offset the protagonist's individualism. Shots pairing him with Eduardo in a party scene at Valentine's Hollywood Hills home or with Jenny's other friend, Elaine, demonstrate that they support Wilson out of loyalty while opposing his criminal violence, as his daughter did when she was alive.

The cinema-verité realism typical of the art film lends an intensity and continuity to Luis Guzman's and Lesley Ann Warren's performances in scenes in which their characters attempt to subvert Wilson's violent plans. By shooting with a scaled-down crew, less equipment, on location, using available light and two handheld cameras within a zone system, the actors were able to move freely without worrying about hitting marks. According to Lachman, this gave them "a feeling of performing in real time and with each other, because the action wasn't cut up into so many pieces" (Williams 58). Lachman and Soderbergh would use this same economical guerilla style of filming even on the much bigger-budget *Erin Brockovich*, and Soderbergh would retain this approach to support actors' performances in *Traffic, Full Frontal, Bubble, Che,* and *The Girlfriend Experience*.

In *The Limey*, such stripped-down realism contributes significantly to a crucial scene between Elaine and Wilson that presents the film's most explicit critique of his plan for revenge. Wilson has been given Elaine's address by Eduardo. When he goes to see her, the scene plays out as they talk by the waterfront, in a restaurant, and finally in her modest garden apartment. We see shots that pair the two characters as they discuss Jenny. "She was magic," Wilson says of his daughter. When their conversation turns to Jenny's mother, Soderbergh cuts away to borrowed footage from Ken Loach's film *Poor Cow*, showing Wilson and his wife many years earlier during happy moments: after lovemaking, in the bath, and walking by a waterfall on a summer day. Yet as the narrative returns to the present and Wilson's plan for revenge, Soderbergh moves from the two-shot compositions back to the singles used earlier in the film; during the ensuing argument, the handheld cameras allow us to see the characters at the moments of greatest intensity:

> ELAINE: What's the deal . . . you and Terry Valentine at twenty paces? Is that it?
> WILSON: Don't see why not . . .
> ELAINE (moving away in disgust): Oh, you fucking guys with your dicks, man!
> WILSON: What do you expect me to do, stay at home doing sweet FA?

As Stamp delivers this last response, he turns to his left, and Soderbergh cuts to the second camera, giving us a better look at his expression (see figure 4). The camera stays on Stamp as the conversation continues:

> ELAINE (offscreen): Terry is never going to give you that satisfaction. . . .
> What makes you so certain?
> WILSON: I bloody ask him.

Figure 4. Wilson determined for revenge. |

The handheld camera then shows us Warren in the bathroom facing out the open door (see figure 5).

ELAINE: Fine, there's the phone. Do you want his number?

Returning to the first camera on Stamp, we see his anger as he responds, "I *got* his number." The scene ends on this line, its double entendre summing up the conflicting ideas of the two characters: Elaine's inclination for dialogue, Wilson's for resolution through violent confrontation.

The following scene offers a similar combination of location settings, handheld camerawork, and available light, this time in support of Eduardo's opposition to Wilson's plan. It opens with the two men shown sitting together in a rental car watching guests arrive at a party at Valentine's luxurious Hollywood Hills home. They squint at the house as Eduardo explains that the men by the front door are parking valets and not "the heavy mob . . . extra muscle" that Wilson mistook them to be. After entering the house and approaching the bar, as if he is James Bond, Wilson asks Eduardo what he'll have from a list of elaborate drinks; but, like the deadpan punchline of a comedy routine, Eduardo looks at the bartender blankly and simply orders a Coke. The subsequent two-shot of

Figure 5. Elaine exasperated with Wilson. |

the men builds on this comic tone as another misunderstanding occurs when Eduardo interprets literally Wilson's Cockney rhyming slang:

WILSON: I'm gonna have a butcher's hook.
EDUARDO: Who are you gonna butcher?
WILSON (impatient at having to explain his meaning): Butcher's hook, look.

The two-shots with Eduardo, marked by the absurdity of their exchange, undercut our expectation that Wilson will unilaterally establish justice; his idiosyncratic manner of speaking subverts his intention rather than communicating it persuasively. Moreover, as Wilson cases the house, we see Eduardo filling his plate from the buffet and awkwardly moving through the party. Clearly, he is not a tough-guy sidekick who will help the outlaw hero impose his will on the situation, and Eduardo makes his opposition to violence overt by blocking Wilson's path when he sees him move menacingly toward Valentine. As during Wilson's conversation with Elaine, the handheld camerawork gives Stamp and Guzman's performances continuity, but it also makes the comic misunderstandings and awkwardness at the party appear less as presentational acting than the absurd reality that underlies the violent justice assumed in this genre story.

Soderbergh's interest in balancing efficient storytelling with expressive characterization and authorial commentary is also evident in the warehouse scene, in which Wilson seeks information about Valentine and receives a hostile reception. This conflict is summed up by an extended take of three young hoods throwing Wilson out, approaching the camera until they are in medium shot. They go back inside, and Wilson gets up, removes a gun from his waistband, and staggers after them. We hear shots from within the warehouse, after which the same long-lens shot shows the lone survivor, a teenage boy, running out and passing by the camera, followed by Wilson, who moves rapidly from a long shot to a medium close-up and yells, "Tell him I'm coming!" To emphasize the intensity of Wilson's rage, Soderbergh pushes in with a handheld camera as the character exits, moving up on Stamp's blood-spattered face and clenched teeth as he emphatically announces the message he wants the boy to deliver (see figure 6).

Figure 6. "Tell him I'm coming!" |

This long take exemplifies Soderbergh's visual style because it shows the conflict at the warehouse clearly and efficiently, yet also concludes with the expressive close-up that encourages the viewer to think critically about Wilson's volatile temper. Independent film is distinguished by its greater average shot length, motivated by the opportunity it provides actors to build their characters. This long take of Wilson's rage is an important part of Terence Stamp's performance in *The Limey*, as it allows him to show the centrality of violence to his character.

In *The Underneath*, important traits of the protagonist Michael's compulsive character and their impact on his relationships with others are shown using long takes that allow us time to look at them carefully. When he turns up unexpectedly to see his ex-wife Rachel two years after abandoning her to escape tens of thousands of dollars in gambling debts, we see them standing together at the bar in a nightclub owned by Rachel's new boyfriend, Tommy, as Michael tells her that he is square with his creditors and she reminds him that he hasn't settled with *her*. Tommy joins them, and the arrangement and actions of the characters in the subsequent thirty-second shot—Michael staring at Rachel, who pretends no interest, and Tommy in the middle looking menacingly at the ex-husband—portends where the story will go: Michael will recklessly pursue Rachel and the money necessary to win her, inattentive to the threat Tommy represents, with Rachel controlling them both. With this long take, Soderbergh shows us these relationships and the future they imply, even as Michael appears oblivious to the ominous signs for his future.

The films (*Sex, Lies, and Videotape, Kafka, King of the Hill, The Underneath,* and later *The Limey*) that established and reaffirmed Soderbergh as a major figure in American independent cinema emphasize characters defined through skilled acting, but longer takes to support such performance are only one part of their eclectic visual style. For example, *The Underneath* relies heavily on fast-paced discontinuity editing to convey the nonlinear nature of Michael's thoughts, moving back and forth between the past and present. Discontinuity editing conveys his confused thinking about the consequences that follow from his destructive actions, as well as his tendency to return to the high-risk behavior that plagued him in the past.

In *Out of Sight,* the need to balance narrative flow with more overt assertions of style prompted Soderbergh to remove a long take from the early scene in which Jack, escaping from prison with the assistance of his friend Buddy, abducts Karen and hides with her in the trunk of a getaway car. Soderbergh originally shot this scene in a single six-minute, thirteen-second take because he wanted to give the audience "emotional proximity" with the desire of the two characters for each other (Kaufman 145). When a version of the film with this long take was shown to a test audience, viewers lost interest at this point in the story. As Soderbergh put it: "It's really hard to find words to describe how derailed the audience became" (DVD commentary). In place of the long take, a new version of the scene was added that cuts away to Buddy driving to maintain the suspense of the escape between close-ups of Karen and Jack as they talk in the trunk.

While he sacrificed a long take for more conventional pacing in the trunk scene, Soderbergh foregrounded visual style to comment on the characters' desire for each other later in the film when Karen and Jack finally meet at a Detroit hotel and make love. Placing this scene nearly two thirds of the way into the film heightens its impact after the long delay required to set up the story, during which the two protagonists engage in long-distance foreplay. Soderbergh begins the love scene with a shot that evokes that psychological buildup by showing Karen's reflection in a window next to her table as she sits in the bar of a Detroit hotel. Foley's reflection soon joins hers, and for a moment we look at a disembodied image of the couple that alludes to the fantasies that have fueled their desire. As Foley sits and they begin talking, the film cuts back and forth in time and space from the couple in the bar to their lovemaking in her room. The thematic continuity of their desire throughout the story—heightened by the danger their relationship represents for both of them—bridges the spatial and temporal fragmentation of the editing. The discontinuity form of this scene also suggests the unorthodox identities of the two main characters: the freeze frames that have marked the frustrations, arrest, and violence in Foley's life earlier in the film recur during their lovemaking and define the relationship as an attempt to, as he puts it, "take a time out" from his merry-go-round of crime and incarceration. In addition to the flash forwards from the bar to lovemaking, a discontinuity device that he borrowed from Nicholas Roeg's 1973 film *Don't Look Now,* Soderbergh also alters the conventional visual logic of sex scenes by showing Clooney's body as much as that of Lopez. As Foley is objectified as what Linda Mizejewski calls "a dangerous man who [is] a woman's sexual fantasy rather than sexual threat," he allows Karen to indulge her desire but remain in control of her professional life (154). In a scene that was cut from the final version but included in the DVD's extra features, her father tells her, "You like the wild ones, Karen."

Soderbergh explained that he wanted to do something to distinguish the sex scene in *Out of Sight* because he thought it would lack interest if he made the physical intimacy too explicit. Yet despite its limited nudity and the fact that, as the editor Anne Coates told Soderbergh, "They [Lopez and Clooney] don't go at it," the unorthodox visual style adds to the eroticism of the scene (DVD commentary). To promote our identification with the couple and give us the "emotional proximity" we couldn't have in the trunk scene, tight framings bring us in close to their attraction, and slow dissolves and the aforementioned freeze frames intensify their foreplay by extending the duration of kisses and embraces.

More than his stylized expression of character subjectivity in *The Underneath, Out of Sight,* and *The Limey,* Soderbergh's use of color upsets the careful balance between Hollywood invisibility and art-film form. As King points out, in mainstream commercial cinema, unconventional form tends to be "restricted to the expression of individual consciousness or experience"; to distort the world at a more objective level runs counter to Hollywood's desire to be generally "affirmative" and "avoid unsettling audiences" (*American Independent* 129). The expressionist chiaroscuro of noir style has been so widely used that its version of visual distortion is one exception to this generalization; the first seventy-seven minutes of *Kafka*, in a high-contrast black and white that invokes an expressionist aesthetic of externalizing government tyranny into the diegetic world, is not a radical formal variation. Yet when that film switches to color in the final sequence, in which the title character, armed with an anarchist's bomb, arrives in the castle to subvert the violent repression he has witnessed, such a strong formal reversal forces the audience to confront the implications of the noir style. This climactic sequence in color shows with greater specificity the sinister scientific apparatus behind the noir symbolism that had stood for how Dr. Murnau (Ian Holm) and his accomplices tortured and altered the brains of those arrested for dissent. After the ominous ambiguity created by the use of chiaroscuro black and white throughout most of the film, the color footage in the castle converts the symbolic menace of the high-contrast noir compositions into the more immediate, tangible threat of Murnau's laboratory. In what Soderbergh has called the "intensified reality" of this color scene, we join the Kafka character to see with greater precision how the tyranny practiced by the authoritarian government through covert violence in the shadows connects to the oppressive scientific investigation and bureaucratic order in the Castle (Kaufman 50).

While the transition from shadowy black and white to vivid color in *Kafka* visualizes the title character's realization of his need to act against the tyranny around him, in several other films Soderbergh's use of color is stylized to express characters' similar assumptions about their world, but also to define narrative space from a nondiegetic—one might say *authorial*—perspective. The green tint when Michael in *The Underneath* involves himself in the armed bank robbery symbolizes the character's desire for money but also how that obsession motivates his destructive behavior. Similarly, the soft, rich yellows and browns of Depression-era St. Louis in *King of the Hill* evoke the optimism rewarded by a WPA job that saves Aaron and his family from eviction. Yet several horrifying images within the soft glow of those colors—Sandoz the artist in a Hooverville, dazed by hunger and hopelessness; the neighbor, Mr. Mungo, slumped over a sink in his room, his wrists slit; and twelve-year-old Aaron by himself, locked in the family apartment to avoid eviction, left to eat pictures of food from a magazine—conflict with the narrative world made gentle and warm by color and available light, emphasizing how these circumstances are incongruent and unjust.

In *Erin Brockovich* and *Traffic*, realism helps validate the portrayal of environmental contamination and illegal drugs, but stylized color allows Soderbergh also to communicate the larger impact of the problems they show. The first film was shot in the town of Hinkley, California, where most of the plantiffs affected by the chromium contamination lived, and many of those victims worked on the film as extras. Soderbergh has commented that, in *Erin Brockovich*, "I very much didn't want to do things that were out of line with the story. . . . Brockovich is such a direct person that I didn't want to get fancy" (Kaufmann 137). Similarly, in *Traffic* Soderbergh took on the job of cinematographer and shot much of the movie with a small crew, handheld camera, and available light to maximize a look of documentary realism. Soderbergh called it his "$45 million dollar Dogme movie" in honor of the Danish avant-garde movement's endorsement of minimalist formal practices (Kaufman 159). He described his attraction to this fast-paced mode of shooting as an "attempt to get at something that feels emotionally honest and immediate" rather than to "polish stuff into oblivion and strangle the life out of a movie" (Kaufman 145, 150).

However, the one aspect of both films that is stylized is the color tone of certain scenes. Because of the generally realist look in *Erin Brockovich*, the bleached-out, seemingly overexposed exterior shots of Hinkley stand out forcefully, visualizing the desiccation of the town, and those who live there, from a lack of clean water. As Erin travels to interview plaintiffs for a class-action suit or clandestinely gathers samples of contaminated water from around the utility company's plant, Hinkley is shown as a dry, desert landscape, its lack of color implying that it is a place now devoid of the life that water sustains.

Likewise, the use of stylized color in *Traffic* is especially forceful because it runs counter to the realist aesthetic of the rest of the movie, contrasting the scenes set in Mexico with those that take place in Cincinnati and Washington, D.C. Soderbergh explained that the Mexican sequences were shot using filters and a forty-five-degree shutter to create a "stroboscopic" effect and were later digitally desaturated to give them a bleached-out, yellowish tint (Kaufman 150). By contrast, those set in Cincinnati and Washington were tinted in blue to suggest the opposing natures of the two places. While Mexico's washed-out light evokes the desolation and poverty that foster the violent business of illegal drugs, the cool blue of D.C. and suburban Cincinnati conversely suggests the detached sense of superiority felt by the politicians and upper-middle-class characters in those locations. But while such tinting distinguishes the contrasting locales, the similarity of their color stylization also implies their affinity; despite their differences, Mexico and the United States are linked in economic and social relationships promoted by globalization, specifically the supply and demand for drugs, as well as the common ineffectualness of both governments in addressing these market forces and the problems of violence and addiction they create.

Experiments in Digital Video:
Full Frontal, K Street, Bubble

In 2002, flush from the blockbuster earnings generated by *Erin Brockovich, Traffic,* and *Ocean's Eleven,* which demonstrated his ability to cross over "from the idiosyncratic into the mainstream," Soderbergh crossed back again with an experiment in digital video (Taylor 1). Ella Taylor explains that the grainy imagery and fragmented story of *Full Frontal* was made possible by the success of his more mainstream projects, which allowed Soderbergh the luxury "to continue doing what he did . . . a decade ago—in other words, whatever he pleases" (2). The three box-office successes also provided Soderbergh with the credibility to support *Full Frontal*'s critique of Hollywood because they demonstrated his ability to succeed within the studio system. As with Robert Altman in *The Player* a decade earlier, Soderbergh's proven track record with stars allowed him to enlist A-list actors to make fun of the ego and artificiality of the movie business. Yet, unlike Altman's film, *Full Frontal* doesn't incorporate the ingredients (suspense, laughter, hope, heart, nudity, sex) that the production-executive protagonist in *The Player* (Tim Robbins) enumerates as necessary to make a commercial film. Instead, Soderbergh used the new digital-video technology to return to his art-film roots, combining realism with character study and authorial statement.

To make *Full Frontal,* Soderbergh chose the Canon XL1S digital-video camera because of its optic image stabilization, which allowed him to shoot most of the film handheld. Such mobility was part of a guerilla aesthetic structured by a Dogme 95–inspired set of rules that stipulated no trailers for actors; no help with their wardrobe, makeup, or hair; no drivers to bring them to locations; and improvisatory performances. Along with the mobile digital-video camera, available light and single takes made it possible to shoot *Full Frontal* in eighteen days (Reed).

The *Variety* reviewer Todd McCarthy criticized *Full Frontal* for its digital-video look: "The visual quality of the digital work is so un-attractive—flared lights, grainy textures, bad balance and unviewable faces abound—that, after the likes of this, *Bamboozled* (2000), *Tadpole* (2002), and most of the Danish Dogme films, one feels like boycotting all further digital-shot theatrical features until further notice." Soderbergh intentionally added the "grainy textures" that displeased McCarthy, de-grading the visual resolution of the 80 percent of *Full Frontal* that is in digital video to heighten its contrast with the remainder that was shot in thirty-five millimeter—a film within the film entitled *Rendezvous* that several of the main characters are making (Reed). Soderbergh explained the purpose of this formal contrast: "I was sort of playing around with perceived notions of aesthetics. Why does chasing somebody around with a DV camera and adopting a documentary style of shooting feel more real than the other sections of the film that are shot on 35mm, in which the camera doesn't move around a lot and cutting is very tradi-tional? Even though they're both fake, why does one feel more real than the other? I was . . . making the audience ask that question" (Reed). The assumptions about documentary style that Soderbergh invokes are those of cinema verité, whereby the mobility of the handheld camera and the use of available light signal an apparent lack of filmmaker involvement to stage those events or improve the image that records them. The documentary filmmaker Errol Morris describes the uncritical audience reaction this style can create: "I think people want the appearance of truth . . . they don't necessarily want the truth" (qtd. in Anderson, "Of Crime," 15). Soderbergh plays on such thinking by using the overt artificiality of *Rendezvous* to make the video portion of *Full Frontal* appear more "real."

While Soderbergh compels viewers to question assumptions that handheld digital video reflects unmediated reality, the lack of image resolution in *Full Frontal* also functions as a metaphor for the blurred identities of the characters, their self-absorption, lack of confidence, or inability to see beyond self-delusion. In both its digital and thirty-five-millimeter formats, *Full Frontal* offers a critical view of the entitlement accepted in Hollywood and of the self-doubt of characters whose lives appear as failures measured against its notion of success. Calvin (Blair Underwood) and Francesca (Julia Roberts) make no apologies for their arrogance and manipulation of others to satisfy their high opinion of themselves, and their roles in *Rendezvous* reflect the same assumptions. In the main story, Catherine Keener plays Lee, a human-resources executive who is having an affair with Calvin and avoids direct discussion with her writer husband, Carl (David Hyde Pierce), about her desire to end their marriage. Despite having written the screenplay for *Rendezvous,* Carl fears that Lee will never see him as a success by Hollywood standards. Lee's sister Linda (Mary McCormack), a massage therapist, also lacks confidence in herself but hopes for a romance with Arty (Enrico Colantoni), whom she met on the Internet. Arty has written and produced an unsuccessful play about Adolph Hitler (*The Sound and the Führer*) that stars a comically self-absorbed actor (Nicky Katt) who can't remember his lines but pretentiously quotes Al Pacino on theories of performance. The lives of these seven characters intersect through a fortieth-birthday-party for *Rendezvous'* producer, Gus (David Duchovny), who dies before the celebration in an accident prompted by his fetish for autoerotic asphyxiation.

This tongue-in-cheek portrayal of artificiality and ego in Hollywood reaches its high point during a scene on a film set, as David Fincher directs Brad Pitt and Underwood as cops pursuing a suspect. After the suspect escapes, Underwood says, "Back to square one. . . . You think different?" Pitt replies, "Like the back of my big ten inch." The uninspired scene we see being filmed and the Pitt character's absurd phallic comment invoke Hollywood's often inflated opinion of its entertainment value, an assumption underscored by the obsession of the producer, Gus, with his own erection and alluded to in the reference to nudity in the title *Full Frontal. Full Frontal* reveals Hollywood's masturbatory fantasy about its ability to provide pleasure for audiences.

As Altman had done in *The Player,* Soderbergh enlisted stars such as Pitt, Roberts, Duchovny, Underwood, Keener, and Fincher to contribute to his sendup of Hollywood. However, *Full Frontal*'s inability to please as well as instruct, its lack of engaging characters and the visual displeasure that McCarthy describes, render it less effective than Soderbergh's hybrid films, which, like *The Player,* use commercial cinema's own sources of appeal to engage the audience while at the same time critiquing Hollywood's obsessive self-interest.

Soderbergh made his second digital-video project, a television series entitled *K Street,* for HBO in 2002. In his attempt to define himself as unafraid to take risks, to pursue innovation, and to aim for high aesthetic standards, Soderbergh has taken an approach similar to that followed by the cable network. Consider the following description by Kim Akass and Janet McCabe of HBO's aesthetic principles: "HBO has instituted a discourse of quality based on creative risk-taking and artistic integrity as well as original tele-literary products that emphasize smart writing, compelling stories told in an innovative way, high production values and a unique creative vision behind each project." Akass and McCabe explain how HBO's approach functions also as a marketing strategy: "Latitude to tell stories differently, creative personnel given the autonomy to work with minimal interference and without having to compromise, has become the HBO trademark—how they . . . sell themselves, how the media talks about them, and how their customers come to understand what they are paying for."

Soderbergh's commitment to experimentation, strong positions on issues, and the creative license his box-office success have afforded him parallel this description of HBO. As with HBO, where not every show has to have a *Sopranos*-sized audience if it builds on the brand identity of aesthetic quality, not everything Soderbergh makes finds a large audience yet for the most part still contributes to his auteur profile of creative integrity and innovation.

Soderbergh directed ten episodes of *K Street.* To speed up shooting, multiple handheld cameras were used, without additional lighting and with sound that was recorded directly during takes. Each of the ten episodes was mapped out at a Monday meeting, shot by Wednesday or

Thursday, and then edited by Soderbergh for delivery to HBO by Friday for airing on Sunday evening.

The series focuses on a Washington, D.C., public-relations and lobbying firm, Bergstrom Lowell, run by two real Beltway insiders: the former Clinton campaign advisor James Carville and his wife, the Republican political consultant Mary Matalin. The other three principal characters are fictional, yet their conflicts and dilemmas seem less contrived because of their constant interaction with actual members of Congress and media personalities. No scripts were used; all the dialogue was improvised. Another level of realism was added by the show's use of current issues: the California governor's race; the presidential campaign of Howard Dean; accusations that Matalin had been involved in leaking the identity of the covert CIA operative Valerie Plane, whose ambassador husband Joseph Wilson had written a report critical of the Bush administration's invasion of Iraq; and the music industry lobbying for legislation to limit illegal downloads.

As in *Full Frontal,* the digital video's lack of image clarity in *K Street* suggests the characters' confusion. Carville and Matalin are blindsided by the FBI's investigation of their firm for funneling money to terrorists through a client, the Council for Mideast Peace. The show's three fictional characters, all staff at Bergstrom Lowell, are also puzzled by the investigation, as well as by the choices they face in their personal lives. Tommy Flanegan (John Slattery) seeks to replicate the relations of power and control that dominate the world of D.C. politics through pornography, prostitutes, and an extramarital affair. As the ten episodes unfold, Maggie Morris (Mary McCormack) becomes increasingly disillusioned about her job as she realizes she's a pawn in a world governed by money and political influence. When asked by her new colleague, Francisco Dupré (Roger G. Smith), what she does for fun, she answers, "I don't play very much," yet her distraction from work grows as she looks for meaning in a failed relationship with Gail (Talia Balsam).

While Maggie pursues emotional intimacy, Francisco's choices of self-definition are inflected by issues of race. He must decide whether to flatter and deceive in order to assert himself as an African American male in a world dominated by assumptions of white superiority. Francisco's conflicting values surface in a scene in which he tells Michael Deaver, a former advisor to Ronald Reagan, that Bob Marley and Reagan share the same birthday and that he views both as inspirational models. The lobbying firm's owner, Richard Bergstrom (Elliot Gould), hires Francisco to undermine the political standing of Carville and Matalin by orchestrating the Council for Middle East Peace scandal. Yet, after two visits to the owner's Brooklyn brownstone, during which Bergstrom spends much of his time watching the 1945 film *Mildred Pierce*, Francisco becomes wary of the role he has been asked to play. Back in Washington, he talks to Tommy about Bergstrom's view of the FBI investigation and how it resembles the Hollywood melodrama: "For him I think it's all just a movie . . . that he can rerun over and over again and be entertained."

The metaphor of blurred vision implied by the low resolution of the digital-video format is reinforced by compositions within the narrative that express the confusion of the characters. In episode 3, a subjective shot shows Tommy's drunken point of view in a bar. He is haunted by hallucinatory sightings of his father's younger wife, Ana (Jennice Fuentes), who committed suicide after she and Tommy had a brief affair. Francisco's ethical dilemma is also visualized by a shot of him in a similarly drunken state in a disco watched by an FBI agent, and in the final episode, after he leaves an NBA game between the Washington Wizards and the Philadelphia 76ers. Approached outside the arena by FBI agents, he appears to reject the Washington establishment in favor of his racial identity. Responding to their questions about the investigation, Francisco refers to a player from the game he has just seen who is known for his "African American" style of play: "[Philadelphia guard Allen] Iverson went for forty [points]." Todd Boyd describes Iverson's ability to play "big" despite his lack of height as representative of his "refusal to accept this fate" (87). Likewise, Francisco doesn't want to give in to the racial barriers in Washington and manipulation by Bergstrom that limit him, but with the investigation closing in, it isn't clear how he can circumvent these obstacles. The subsequent scene shows his indecision through the motif of vision: Francisco exits a cab without knowing where he is headed, and the episode ends on a shot looking out through the vehicle's rain-splattered window.

Besides these uses of visual form to imply the characters' conflicted subjectivities, Soderbergh also juggles the narrative chronology to comment on the meaning of events. In episode 4, the story jumps back three months to show Francisco going to Brooklyn to be hired by Bergstrom. Arriving in New York in a cab, we see him looking at a newspaper ad for the Arnold Schwarzenegger film *Terminator 3*, and later we overhear Maggie and Gail discussing the California governor Grey Davis's faltering campaign against the movie star. Other scenes in episode 4 show Francisco watching news coverage of the California governor's campaign and Tommy talking on the phone with a candidate about a marketing campaign aimed at swing voters—"We're going as wide as possible . . . through Labor Day," he says, as if describing the type of saturation advertising typical of a blockbuster film like *Terminator 3*, timed to run during the summer season when big Hollywood movies typically make the most money. In her review of *K Street*, Amy Taubin notes how, in contrast to most television-news coverage of politics that avoids suggesting any connection between stories, the complexity of Soderbergh's series leaves us no choice but to assemble its narrative puzzle. The various closely placed allusions to politics and to Hollywood film suggest the similarities between the two, particularly their overemphasis on charismatic star personalities and advertising. Soderbergh uses allusion to support this parallel, both in his invocation of *Terminator 3* and through the use of *Mildred Pierce* to characterize Bergstrom. As the latter film is about manipulation to pursue self-interest, Bergstrom practices the same actions in the political world, suggesting a parallel between deception in the fictional narratives of Hollywood films and in American politics.

However, the apparently strong, "heroic" personalities that sell well in Hollywood blockbusters and American politics are shown in *K Street* to be more about artifice and appearance than substance. Soderbergh begins the first four episodes with careful attention to the look of wealth and success necessary in Washington: as episode 1 opens, we see Francisco getting his shoes shined and his hair cut and picking out expensive clothes before he first arrives at Bergstrom Lowell. Episode 2 starts at a concert by Branford Marsalis at the luxurious Four Seasons hotel in Washington, attended by an affluent audience in formal wear. Episode 3 begins with a shot of Tommy's Acura, and 4 opens with Matalin and Carville discussing the new décor of their offices as they tell the designers they want "a money fabric" and a "power color . . . let's make people pay a bigger fee." Taubin comments that the most disturbing aspect of *K Street* is how the politicians and other Washington insiders like Carville and Matalin seem so convincing in fictional situations, showing their skill at appearing in control of the truth even when they are inventing it.

While in several ways *K Street* highlights the similarities between his career and the aesthetic principles and business plan for HBO, Soderbergh's penchant for allusion belies the promise of uniqueness offered by the network's "Original Programming" slogan. *K Street's* mix of fiction with real people and situations is not new; in fact, it evokes the combination of the two in other HBO programs, such as *Curb Your Enthusiasm,* which uses improvised dialogue and people playing themselves, and the actual politicians and fictional characters in the HBO series *Tanner,* set during the 1988 Democratic Primary. Carville and Matalin also were not newcomers to performing for the camera, as both had appeared in D. A. Pennebaker's 1992 documentary about the Bill Clinton presidential campaign, *The War Room* (Taubin).

Soderbergh even used *K Street* as an opportunity to allude to his own work. The blue tinting of several scenes in which Carville, Matalin, and members of Congress pronounce on political issues recalls the use of color stylization in *Traffic* to suggest the cool self-assurance of entitled Americans in contrast to the yellowish hue for the scenes set in Mexico. In fact, the whole idea for *K Street* seemed to grow out of the Georgetown cocktail-party scene in *Traffic,* in which Washington politicians (including Senators Orrin Hatch and Barbara Boxer, who appear in both the 2000 film and the HBO series), lobbyists, and media figures proclaim their positions on illegal narcotics to the drug czar Bob Wakefield.

Like *Full Frontal* and *K Street,* Soderbergh's 2006 motion picture *Bubble* employs a realist aesthetic based in digital video to show characters struggling to negotiate difficult social environments. The friction between characters in *Full Frontal* and *K Street* is a direct result of the ethos of power and money that operates in Hollywood and inside the Beltway. Likewise, in *Bubble,* the attempts by Rose to manipulate Kyle (Dustin Ashley) and Martha (Debbie Doebereiner) replicate the exploitation experienced by all three characters in the workplace. Shot on location in the small southeastern Ohio town of Belpre, just across the river from West Virginia, *Bubble* shows the three characters working at a doll factory and the murder that results when their alienated lives put them in conflict. In addition to digital video, available light, location shooting, and improvisatory performance, Soderbergh went a step beyond the realism of *Full Frontal* and *K Street* by using only nonprofessional actors in *Bubble*. He was able to get naturalistic performances by not requiring memorized dialogue that might make them self-conscious, allowing the novice actors instead to speak in their own voices while following a general narrative outline.

Soderbergh also sought to reduce as much as possible the artificiality of the performance situations by using very little equipment and a small crew. He describes this kind of direction as creating an environment as close to real life as possible, so that actors can "stop performing and just behave" as they do in real life (Gross). In addition, the lower cost of allowing a digital-video camera to run, even if the footage wasn't ultimately used, reduced the pressure on the novice actors. This approach worked remarkably well in the scene in which Decker Moody, an actual police detective from the area in which the story takes place, interrogates Martha about her involvement in Rose's murder. Soderbergh explained that only he and another camera operator were present during this scene and that no discussion had taken place with Doebereiner as to what questions she would be asked or how she would respond. In the shot that shows Martha answering Moody's gradually more direct questions about her guilt, we see distress appear on her face. Doebereiner explained that not knowing what would happen during the scene and seeing graphic photos of Rose's body upset her and helped generate the emotions. While Hollywood films generally only feature working-class characters—like Julia Roberts in *Erin Brockovich* or as a prostitute in *Pretty Woman*—as they show the strength to improve their social status, this shot sums up how the circumstances of Martha's life have created anger and frustration that the conflict with Rose brought out in self-destructive violence. *Bubble* ends with a similar, if less emotionally charged, close-up shot of Kyle standing alone in the shovel factory where he works a second job, apparently thinking about the experience of the two women. Rather than optimistic upward mobility, *Bubble* shows working-class characters puzzled and isolated as they attempt to respond to economic exploitation.

In addition to a guerilla digital-video shooting style to enhance the realism of the performances, Soderbergh added verisimilitude by leaving many of the scenes in *Full Frontal*, *K Street*, and *Bubble* unresolved. This lack of resolution might be explained in the case of the HBO series by the fact that it was canceled after only ten episodes. But in the two feature films, such open-endedness departs from the Hollywood convention of concluding a scene before the cause for its events has been fully shown, only to return to provide an explanation later as part of a pattern that maintains viewer curiosity while weaving the parts of the story into a tighter whole. We never see in *Bubble* what Rose does to provoke Martha, where Francisco goes after he leaves the cab as *K Street* ends, or what happens with the relationship between Linda and Arty in *Full Frontal*. Such incompleteness fits an art-film notion of realism, in which the assumption is that "life is more complex than art can ever be, and . . . the only way to respect this complexity is to leave causes dangling and questions unanswered" (Bordwell, "Authorship and Narration" 43).

Besides his affinities with HBO at the level of innovation and creative freedom, *Bubble* also exemplifies Soderbergh's acceptance of a convergent distribution strategy like that adopted by the network to make its programming available across media platforms. Responding to "how people consume media these days," HBO set up view-on-demand access to programming for what Akass and McCabe call "income rich, time poor" consumers who want to watch shows at a time they choose, to go along with box sets and programming available for download to mobile devices. Out of a similar interest in increasing audience access, Soderbergh approached Todd Wagner's and Mark Cuban's 2929 production company to finance *Bubble*. Wagner and Cuban began investing in film production in 2001, two years after selling their streaming-video site Broadcast.com to Yahoo for $5.7 billion. Their ownership of the Landmark Theater chain and the HDNet cable-television network made it possible, as part of a day-and-date strategy of release, for viewers to see *Bubble* in a theater, on cable television, or on DVD on the date of its release (Hornaday). Soderbergh explained that this distribution strategy was intended to increase the availability of the film to viewers who may not live close to a Landmark theater—the chain has fifty-nine locations in twenty-three cities—and to eliminate the usual cost of multiple advertising campaigns (one for theatrical release and one for the DVD) and to help eliminate piracy (Gross). While *K Street* refers to the importance of saturation advertising for blockbuster films and major political campaigns, by contrast, art films like *Bubble* need to use less expensive strategies such as day-and-date to maximize their exposure to audiences. In a May 2006 panel discussion at the Tribeca Film Festival, Soderbergh emphasized the reduced costs of day-and-date by noting that advertising and the cost of making thirty-five-millimeter prints had risen 110 percent in the previous decade (Silverman). Besides controlling marketing and distribution costs, addressing the issue of copyright is also important to small films, where profit margins, if they exist at all, have no room to absorb revenue lost to piracy. In this sense, one statement by a Washington insider in *K Street* rings true. Commenting on the music industry's concern about illegal downloading, Utah Senator Orrin Hatch states, "If you don't protect the rights of those who are creating . . . they're not going to create."

Even with its increased viewing options, *Bubble* generated only modest revenues, yet Soderbergh's use of the day-and-date release strategy has been part of a bigger pattern for American independent filmmakers who are looking for new forms of distribution. John Sayles and David Lynch have begun using multiple forms of distribution in response to a marketplace in which, according to Manohla Dargis, "movies are whisked off screens so fast that it's hard for audiences to discover them. . . . [T]hese days, too many cool movies are just passing though on the way to your Netflix queue" (14). The maketing plan for Sayles's 2007 film *Honeydripper*, about a 1950s blues club, involved "a forward-looking synthesis of digital projection, colleges, blues bars, underserved movie houses, and the Internet." For his part, Lynch has taken to self-distributing largely through a Web site (Anderson, "Down South," 14).

At the corporate level, the CEO of Netflix, Reed Hastings, called Soderbergh's use of day-and-date "encouraging news," as his company moved toward collapsing the release window by offering movies via streaming video (Zeitchik). Conversely, theater owners in the United States, who had seen a 5 percent decline in box office in 2005, responded negatively to Soderbergh's experiment. The film director M. Night Shyamalan also regarded the day-and-date strategy as a threat to the social experience of public film viewing. "'When I sit down next to you in a movie theater . . . we become part of a collective soul,'" he said. "'That's the magic in the movies'" (qtd. in Hornaday). Soderbergh responded to Shyamalan by commenting, "'I really don't care how people see my movies, as long as they see them. I'm just not interested in controlling how somebody experiences one of my films'" (qtd. in Hornaday).

The strategy for *Bubble* of combining lower production and marketing costs with day-and-date distribution prompted Ann Hornaday to describe the project as "the most visible example of an emerging model that could seismically shift the way Hollywood does business." Soderbergh himself made equally provocative statements at the Tribeca Film Festval panel, saying that "the economic model of the film business is broken" and proclaiming the need to "redesign [Hollywood] from scratch" (Silverman).

The politics of class implicit in Soderbergh's films, made more overt by his biopic of the Latin American Marxist revolutionary Ernesto "Che" Guevara, would suggest an interest in the creative workers in the media industry taking control of the means of production. However, despite Soderbergh's experiments with new technology to support a restructuring of the economic relations of the media industry, the creative pragmatism demonstrated by his synthesis of Hollywood genre and stars with art-film auteurism is matched by a similar willingness to work within the entertainment business to change it. Qualifying his more radical statements about the need to overhaul the industry, he has also urged sharing of revenue with theater owners as movies are increasingly released on new platforms so that greater availability won't limit the aesthetic and social experiences they offer. Although Todd Wagner at the Tribeca panel discussion noted that ticket sales in 2005 made up only 13 percent of Hollywood revenue, his partner Mark Cuban has also acknowledged that "no matter how big a home theater you have, its not a cure for cabin fever" (Silverman; Mohr). As further evidence of Soderbergh's willingness to work from inside the Hollywood system to change it, he served as vice president of the Directors Guild, which came to an agreement in January 2008 with the Alliance of Motion Picture and Television Producers on a new contract, using the pressure of the writers' strike to get producers to improve the rate directors are paid for electronic sell-through of their work (Littleton).

Class Conflict in High Definition:
Che and *The Girlfriend Experience*

The overt emphasis on class conflict in Soderbergh's 2009 biopic of Che Guevara marks a departure not from the topic itself, which has been a consistent theme in his movies, but from his past practice of submerging it within genre stories. However, consistent with his pragmatic tendency to downplay in public comments the political positions of his work, the director insisted, "I didn't make the movie because I'm in sync with him [Guevara] politically" (Garrett). He explained instead that the four-and-a-half-hour, two-part film is simply "an attempt to re-create a piece of history" (Ressner 2). Because of the story's focus on Guevara's leadership in the armed insurgency to overthrow the Cuban dictator Fulgencio Batista and his subsequent attempt to export revolution to the rest of Latin America, Soderbergh employed a guerilla style of filmmaking, using available light and real locations in Spain, Puerto Rico, Bolivia, New York, and Mexico, shooting with the lightweight (five kilogram) Red One digital-video camera that is close to thirty-five-millimeter film in image quality. Besides adopting an agile visual style appropriate to the film's subject, Soderbergh worked to ensure the accuracy of his historical film by reading widely on the subject, talking to, as he put it, "almost everyone alive who knew Che well" and employing the journalist Jon Lee Anderson, whose 1997 book on Guevara is the definitive biography in English and who discovered the site of Che's burial in Bolivia, as the film's principal advisor (Sterritt interview in this volume).

Robert Rosenstone has written that, while historians often question their completeness and accuracy, movies have the potential to represent aspects of the past more effectively than written texts (15). This is clearly Soderbergh's assumption in his emphasis in *Che* on what Dennis Lim calls "the concrete minutiae and tactile experience" of Guevara's activities as a guerilla fighter (4). The screenwriter Peter Buchman has stated that Soderbergh "'wanted it to feel like we were looking over their shoulders, like you're in the jungle with those guys'" (qtd. in Lim 4). This materialist quality is underlined when *Che* begins and ends with close-ups of combat boots, a framing device that Anthony Lane has interpreted as demonstrating "Soderbergh's desire to shoot at ground level—not to linger on the loftiness of political ideals, [but] to get down amid the dirt, sweat, and despair of putting them into practice" (72).

Several critics and interviewers questioned the morality of what they regarded as Soderbergh's favorable portrayal of Che. For example, the interviewer David Sterritt calls Guevara "a violent revolutionary who killed an awful lot of people" (interview in this volume). Soderbergh responded that rather than champion revolutionary violence, he wanted to acknowledge how Che "put his life on the line for people he didn't know," and show his "extreme level of engagement" on behalf of those less fortunate than himself (Sterritt interview in this volume; Garrett). When asked what links Che with the outsider characters in his other films, Soderbergh described them all as "protagonists who try, through sheer force of will, to influence what happens to them and their surroundings" (Garrett).

But when pressed on Che's violence, in particular the executions he oversaw after Batista's government had been overthrown, Soderbergh responded that, in his view, the Cuban revolutionary government—in reaction to attempts by the United States and Cuban exiles to undermine it—reacted in the same "excessive manner" that any regime would have "when it feels threatened" (Sterritt interview in this volume). Soderbergh also explained the violence of the Cuban Revolution and Che's attempts to export it as prompted by U.S. imperialism in Latin America: "You have to consider the context in which he lived, the conditions in that part of the world, at that point in time, when every country in the Caribbean and Latin America was run by a leader in the pocket of the United States, and they were being used as machines to make money for the U.S." (Sterritt interview in this volume).

Despite these statements in defense of Che, Soderbergh's film generally concerns itself more with Guevara's strong sense of duty to the disadvantaged. While the scenes of his trip to the United Nations in 1964 in part 1 include some of Che's statements against North American imperialism and in support of the Cuban people's right to sovereignty, for the most part Benicio Del Toro's performance is less about proclamations of ideology than repeated representation of self-sacrifice. We see Che the trained physician giving medical care to wounded guerillas and rural peasants who have never seen a doctor, fighting shoulder to shoulder with his men for months at a time despite asthma attacks and a lack of food, and even once the revolution is won and he has a prominent place in the new government, Guevara gives up his life of comfort and authority and dies in an attempt to export the revolution to Bolivia. Like the rhyming image of boots that underlines the film's materialist emphasis, Che's belief in the need for revolution throughout Latin America—Anderson quotes a 1959 speech in which Guevara stated that "'the Revolution is not limited to the Cuban nation'" (393)—also bookends the film. The movie begins with his first meeting with Fidel Castro in 1955, at which he tells the Cuban leader that the injustices that necessitate revolution in Cuba exist throughout Latin America. A flashback at the film's conclusion returns to the same conversation, as Castro asks if Che will join the fight, and he responds: "Only if after Cuba you let me bring the revolution to all Latin America."

Besides film's ability to bring life to the written word, Rosenstone notes that historical movies can show "the social and political concerns of the era in which they were made" (48). When asked about the importance of *Che* today, Soderbergh responded that Guevara's "dream of a classless society, a society that isn't built on the profit motive, is still relevant" (Ressner 1). This comment responds to Anthony Lane's assertion that one of the ironies of *Che* is that Guevara's "bourgeois profession [medicine] may have done more practical good . . . than his wild proletarian ardor" (74). The flaw in Lane's logic is his assumption that, without some form of "proletarian ardor," the poor would even have access to doctors. Made at a time when, even in the United States— let alone Latin America—tens of millions of people lacked access to health care, the impassioned fight in *Che* against profit at the expense of peoples' lives is still valid.

At first glance, *The Girlfriend Experience,* Soderbergh's second digital-video project in his six-picture deal with Todd Wagner's and Mark Cuban's 2929 Productions, appears very different from *Che*—another example of Soderbergh's taste for variety. Compared to the $1.7 million budget for *The Girlfriend Experience, Che* cost seventy million dollars to make, involved dialogue mostly in Spanish, a large cast, locations in five countries, and pressure on Soderbergh to negotiate the conflicting historical assessments of Guevara—a working-class hero for some and a totalitarian murderer to others. *The Girlfriend Experience* is a much smaller story in scope, a case study of Chelsea (Sasha Grey), a high-priced escort working in Manhattan.

Yet the two films share certain traits. Both were shot on location with available light and the same portable Red One digital-video camera, using the guerilla style that has become increasingly prominent in Soderbergh's work since *Traffic*. The two movies also both address issues of economic inequality and the power of money, although *The Girlfriend Experience* follows the pattern in most of Soderbergh's films of embedding class conflict within stories of individual alienation and transgression. While *Che* shows Guevara's leadership of violent revolution against moneyed interests in Latin America, *The Girlfriend Experience* focuses on how rich clients buy intimacy, not only from escorts like Chelsea but from workers in a service sector of the economy that includes "therapists, exercise instructors [like Chelsea's boyfriend Chris], nannies, manicurists, bartenders . . . all paid for something that can easily be mistaken for love" (Scott). As in *Che, The Girlfriend Experience* divides characters along class lines, although, like the three doll-factory workers at the center of *Bubble,* Chelsea and Chris demonstrate little understanding of how their identities are influenced by these economic forces. When not meeting clients, we see Chelsea emulating the entrepreneurial behavior her customers talk to her about, strategizing about how to build her escort business. Likewise, Chris travels to Las Vegas with a group of wealthy clients on a private jet and listens as they discuss their deals, seemingly unaware that their attraction to his youth and athleticism, presented as friendship, is as performative and self-interested as the attention he gives them at the health club.

The first half of *Che* celebrates Guevara's success in the Cuban Revolution as the result—like the legal victory led by Erin Brockovich—of convincing those he was fighting for of his commitment and concern for their interests. The latter half of the biopic, however, shows that Guevara's tragic failure to win hearts and minds in Bolivia led to his death. Conversely, in *The Girlfriend Experience,* characters who lack awareness of what causes and how to respond to their alienation can only attempt to exploit and profit from the similar dissatisfaction of others.

Music and Authorship in *Ocean's Eleven* and *The Limey*

Soderbergh has described his combination of Hollywood genre with "'a European film aesthetic'" as "'pretending we're in the late '60s and early '70s'" (qtd. in Biskind 23). Seen within this historical line of influence, the continuous tendencies in his career as a director all appear to come out of the New American Cinema to which he pays homage: his pursuit of a middle ground resembles the ambition of auteurs like Arthur Penn, Martin Scorsese, Francis Ford Coppola, and Robert Altman to change

Hollywood from within without upsetting the long-held assumptions of narrative, the star system, and profits; his interest in discontinuity and self-reflexivity recall the influence of the French New Wave on U.S. cinema during that period; and his use of allusion matches the broader knowledge of film history characteristic of the first generation of American directors to have gone to film school.

To sum up my argument about the formal and thematic continuities in Soderbergh's films, allow me to conclude with a brief analysis of the music in *The Limey*—a movie representative of his role in defining an independent aesthetic as well as his debt to the New American Cinema— and *Ocean's Eleven,* a remake full of A-list stars and an example of his most commercially successful work. Although the nondiegetic music in these two apparently so different films is certainly not part of the realist tendency of his formal style, it demonstrates Soderbergh's persistent concerns with expressive characterization, allusion, self-reflexivity, and discontinuity in the service of authorial commentary, all within a narrative framework.

In the opening scene of *The Limey,* a close-up of Wilson arriving at Los Angeles International Airport from London in search of his daughter's killer is accompanied by the Who's 1970 single "The Seeker." With this juxtaposition, Soderbergh establishes the centrality and the nature of Wilson's character. Through the aggressive tone established by Pete Townsend's percussive guitar, the intensity of Roger Daltrey's vocals, and the lyrics themselves—"People tend to hate me / 'Cause I never smile / As I ransack their homes / They want to shake my hand"—Soderbergh presents the alienation, violence, and criminality that are the back story for Stamp's character.

Once Wilson arrives by cab at a nondescript motel near the airport, we see several shots of him thinking—in his room, but also jumping back and forth in time, on the plane, in the taxi, and as he subsequently hears the circumstances of his daughter's death from her friend, Eduardo, intercut with images of Jenny. As the discontinuity editing in this sequence visualizes the nonlinear patterns of Wilson's memory, we begin to hear the sound of running water—an aural metaphor for the flow of his thoughts—and then the faint sound of chimes, as if he is lost in solitary reverie in his garden.

Cliff Martinez's score works with the discontinuity editing to characterize Wilson in terms of memory and loss while also advancing the narrative as he pursues revenge. As we continue to watch him thinking, juxtaposed with images of Jenny, alternating notes rise on the sound track, soon followed by a series of oblique piano chords. As strings join the piano, the music becomes more clearly narrative, suggesting conflict and creating suspense, and the story moves forward: we see Wilson buy a gun in an East L.A. park and travel to a seemingly empty warehouse district, reinforcing our intuition that the violence the music has implied will soon take place. Even as the previous alternating notes on the piano expand into a more regular pattern of four pairs of notes played repeatedly, random notes remain, suggesting with their apparent lack of direction the play of memory that dominated the previous sequence, reminding us of Wilson's thoughts and recollections motivating the dangerous action he is about to undertake.

Yet, a subsequent series of fragmented shots, combined with music and cinematic allusion, portend the failure of Wilson's plan for revenge. Another shot of him smoking in his motel is accompanied by Wilson humming the Donovan song "Colours," which Stamp had performed in *Poor Cow* (dir. Ken Loach, 1967), in which he played the same character, then a young tough, who is arrested for robbery and goes to jail. This allusion to Loach's film at several points in *The Limey* adds to our understanding of Stamp's character and his life of crime, especially in the final scene when, after having tracked down Jenny's killer, we see Wilson returning to England. Seated on the plane, he remembers a scene from *Poor Cow* in which, as a young man, he had performed "Colours" with his acoustic guitar for Jenny's mother. He sang:

Freedom is a word I rarely use without thinking, mm hmm
Without thinking, mm hmm
Of the time, of the time
When I was loved.

This verse communicates that revenge has not adequately compensated Wilson for the relationship with his daughter he has lost by spending much of his adult life in jail. Instead, using Donovan's song, he can only escape briefly into the memory of a happier time before his imprisonment. Soderbergh's construction of Wilson's individual and social identities through memory—presented using discontinuity editing and Martinez's score, combined with musical and cinematic allusion—results in a self-reflexive rejection of Hollywood's conventional outlaw hero who employs violence to establish a personal sense of justice and moral order.

The fact that Terence Stamp's Wilson in *The Limey* and George Clooney's title character in *Ocean's Eleven* have so much in common—both are lifelong thieves who have just gotten out of prison and are after revenge against the rich who benefit from the status quo that has kept them down—suggests the ideological continuity between these two films. Yet the presence of Clooney, Brad Pitt, Julia Roberts, and the film's eighty-five-million-dollar production budget also implies that the political statements in *Ocean's Eleven* will be made less through discontinuity form than more subtle self-reflexivity.

This self-reflexivity serves to communicate the class tensions Soderbergh sets up between Danny Ocean, his crew of thieves, and their mark, Benedict. The plot partly conceals such social difference behind a love triangle whereby Ocean's motivation for robbing Benedict comes from the fact that he is dating the thief's ex-wife, Tess. Yet the use of David Holmes's smooth jazz/funk compositions to introduce and convey a self-assured urban cool that encourages viewer identification with the two main perpetrators of the heist, Ocean and Brad Pitt's Rusty Ryan, also hint at the class politics involved.

To help establish the film's statement against corporate entertainment, these introductory scenes juxtapose the two characters against architectural monuments of American mass culture: in the case of Ocean, the Trump Casino in Atlantic City, and for Ryan, the Capitol Records building in Hollywood (see figures 7 and 8). Yet the characters' confidence and cool, and the music that introduces them, work to dispel any doubt about their eventual success. What Soderbergh and Holmes aim for here is an example of what the composer George Antheil describes when he states that "'the characters in a film drama never know what is going to happen to them, but the music always knows'" (qtd. in Maltby 461). To support the music's suggestion of a positive outcome for these two thieves, in these introductory scenes we see them winning at games of chance: Ocean in his first hand of blackjack in an Atlantic City casino,

Figures 7 and 8. Monuments of Mass Culture:
Trump Casino in Atlantic City and the
Capitol Records Building in Hollywood.

and both men together as they scam young actors whom Pitt's character
is teaching to play poker.

This inference of success for Ocean and Ryan, aided by the music
in these early scenes, allows Soderbergh to focus on the core values
of his filmmaking style: character and a critical self-refexivity. He uses
the first thirty minutes to set up each of the eleven members of the
crew, as Holmes's loping jazz and jazz/rock selections do double duty,
at times adding to the characterization and also motoring forward the
film's drawn-out exposition. This introductory sequence concludes with
a pop-music reference appropriate to the setting that also pokes fun at
the priority thus far given to characterization founded on dialogue and
performance. With a dramatic helicopter shot, the narrative arrives in
Las Vegas to Elvis Presley singing "a little less conversation, a little more

action / Come along with me, put your mind at ease." These lyrics not only poke fun at the movie's slow pacing to that point but also articulate the underlying assumption that such a high-rolling film should cover its bets with more plot and invisible style.

After a film full of jazz and funk, it is incongruous that *Ocean's Eleven's* penultimate scene, as we see Ocean's reunion with Tess and then the other thieves gathering to watch the Bellagio's fountain display in celebration of a successful heist, is set to the sounds of Claude Debussy's *Clair de lune*. Although its lyrical use of oboe and harp fit the constitution of the romantic couple, Debussy's music provides more ironic counterpoint than conventional classical score as the camera tracks across the faces of the ten thieves and, one by one, each turns his back on the casino and leaves, the last punctuated by the amplified sound of the jets of water we see with the Bellagio behind them, so that they sound like the explosions that the crew used to blow the vault and destablize this monument to corporate profit.

While it is certainly easier to recognize the impact of *The Limey's* up-front distanciation founded upon discontinuity editing, Cliff Martinez's modernist music, and pop cues with a social conscience, I want to be so bold as to suggest that ultimately *Ocean's Eleven* is just as political. As Frederick Wasser rightly states, "[T]he once popular analysis of the link between politics and cinematic form that argued the jump cut a blow against capitalism" has to make room for other kinds of political filmmaking ("Political Polarization"). My argument on behalf of Soderbergh's hybrid style of filmmaking as it is exemplified by *Ocean's Eleven* may sound like little more than a nostalgic longing for the high production values and wry sophistication common in classic Hollywood. Yet, as compromised as that film is by the imperatives of its global profit expectations, *Ocean's Eleven* also represents an important step back from the extremity that has characterized the recent dominance of American blockbuster filmmaking. Writing in the *New York Times* in 2004, Lynn Hirschberg states that "[w]hen you look at the big international hits . . . it is easy to understand why the world views America with a certain disgust. . . . American films used to be an advertisement for life in the States—there was sophistication, depth, the allure of a cool, complex manner." Hirschberg also quotes a studio executive who says that Hollywood blockbusters are "distorted exaggerations. And I think America's growing into those exaggerated images." Certainly Soderbergh's art films reject the violence and adolescent obsessions of so much recent Hollywood filmmaking, yet even his movies with greater audience appeal aren't afraid to ask viewers to fill in the blanks and consider complex issues. When almost a half-century ago Andrew Sarris claimed that the brilliance of John Ford and Alfred Hitchcock was evident in their ability to work within yet also to transcend the Hollywood studio system, his goals were to raise the cultural status of movies in general and claim preeminence for his pantheon of directors in particular. As America looks to right itself and emerge from a period of arrogance, violence, and greed reflected in the "exaggerated images" of the Hollywood blockbuster, the stakes today may be even higher.

Interviews with Steven Soderbergh |

The two interviews selected for this volume offer insights into several of the most prominent aspects of Steven Soderbergh's career as a filmmaker. The first interview, Geoff Andrew talking with Soderbergh and George Clooney before a live audience in London in 2003, touches on remakes, allusion, and their collaboration with the aim, in the actor's words, "to push the things we've learned from foreign and independent films . . . back into the studio system."

The second interview, conducted by David Sterritt, focuses on *Che*, probably Soderbergh's most ambitious film to date. After acknowledging Soderbergh's tendency to experiment and defy expectations, Sterritt in his introduction calls *Che* "a daring project even for him." What follows in the interview is the director's defense of the politics of class, embedded in all his films, that came to the forefront in *Che*. Soderbergh ends the interview by paralleling Guevara's political engagement with his own attempt to truthfully represent social realities in his films: "If you make any film that accurately portrays the world as it is, that portrays people's lives the way they actually are, by definition that's a political film."

Interview with Steven Soderbergh and George Clooney

(By Geoff Andrew. *The Guardian*, February 13, 2003)

GEOFF ANDREW: Back in 1989, I met a twenty-six-year-old whose film was just about to play at the Cannes Film Festival. He went on to win the Palm d'Or with *Sex, Lies, and Videotape*. When I spoke to him around the time he made *Traffic*, he told me that he was going to remake *Solaris*. I said, "Are you crazy?" He didn't tell me who he was going to put in the film. It is a rather fine film, and one of the bravest, most audacious and intelligent films to come out of any American studio in several decades. It's not an easy film, but it's really something special.

First, I'd like to thank George and Steven for coming along and doing this *Guardian* interview and allowing us this special screening of *Solaris*, which I think is quite a special film, and which I'd like to ask you about. Then I'll ask you about some of the other films you've made, and about setting up Section Eight together.

Let's start with Steven. You had a suggestion from a friend at Fox that you might like to make a sci-fi film, and you decided to do *Solaris*. What exactly was the appeal of doing *Solaris* again?

STEVEN SODERBERGH: Well, I guess memory was an issue that I dealt with a couple of times before, and this seemed to be a very interesting way of talking about memory—having a character that was a physical manifestation of someone's memory seemed like a very intriguing idea to me. And I wasn't at all of a mind that the Tarkovsky film could be improved upon; I thought there was a very different interpretation to be had. The analogy that I use was that the Lem book, which was full of so many ideas that you could probably make a handful of films from it, was the seed, and that Tarkovsky generated a sequoia, and we were sort of trying to make a little bonsai. And that was really what we were doing. I took a very specific aspect of the book and tried to expand Rheya's character and bring her up to the level of Kelvin.

GA: Did you feel it was risky making such a cerebral film, perhaps one of the most uncompromisingly audacious films produced by a studio in the last two or three decades? Did you ever think, Oh my God, what am I doing this for?

SS: In the past couple of weeks that we've been traveling around talking about the film, there've been a lot of questions about commercial films and noncommercial films, and I've never really made that separation in my mind. There's no question that when you read a piece of material, you have ideas about how it should be realized. Certainly, when I read the script for *Ocean's Eleven*, I thought if this was realized the way it should, then it would appeal to a lot of people. Then you get involved in a film like *Solaris*, and if you realize it the way it should be realized, then it won't appeal to a lot of people. But what are you going to do? You have to go at it, and we've been lucky enough that Fox was supportive and let us have our way. You know, if you don't take advantage and take those opportunities to do something when things are on the upswing, then I don't know what you're doing.

GA (to George Clooney): Steven didn't write the part with you in mind; you wanted to be in it. It's a rather laconic role and a difficult film, which is full of grief and confusion. Why did you want to do it?

GEORGE CLOONEY: I'm full of grief and confusion myself. There's a bunch of reasons: first, because I read the script, and let's face it, you get to the position I'm in and read the amount of screenplays that I do, there aren't that many good screenplays out there. First and foremost as an actor, you want to work with a good screenplay. Then, also, you feel like it's a really uncompromising film that's got to be done within a studio. We've been trying to push our involvement within the studio system, sort of push the things that we've learned from foreign and independent films through the eighties and push those things back into the studio system. Like *Out of Sight* isn't your standard studio film by any means; *Three Kings* wasn't the standard Warner Brothers kind of film. And this one seemed like it was really going to push it. And I liked the idea that Steven was raising a lot of questions that he was trying to work out himself, and I thought it would really be fun to go on that run with him. You can trust a director like Steven with that kind of risk. I wouldn't have done this with some directors, who shall remain nameless.

GA: It must have been quite difficult playing so many scenes where you're not quite sure whether they're real or remembered or imagined or dreamed. How do you play that? Did Steven give you any direction?

GC: No, he didn't direct. Let's face it, I did this all by myself. Um, I'd just the week before finished principal photography on *Confessions* [*of a Dangerous Mind*], which was a long, hard shoot, and I'd set up an editing bay at Warner Brothers, and I was literally shooting on the set for thirteen to fourteen hours a day and then editing for three to four hours a night and sleeping in the trailer lot. And I thought that it would work to my advantage, the fact that I was physically tired. All you really do is show up on the set and try not to have any of those barriers or those crutches that actors have. And with this, there were none of those crutches—there weren't that many other actors, there was no humor in it, there aren't the things that you can usually hide behind. And you just show up and let Steven say, "Okay, it's the last thirteen seconds of your life—go!" And trust him when he says, "Okay, now 20 percent more existential grief." So again, it comes down to trust. If you're lucky enough to work with people you trust . . . like, I've just finished another film with the Coen brothers. You just have to trust those guys, because their work has been consistently sticking their necks out, like Steven's is. And because you also know him and what he's trying to do.

GA: And they're even more enigmatic directors than Steven, presumably. They don't really talk to anybody apart from themselves, a lot of the time.

GC: Yeah, with them, you know you're going the right way when you hear [makes honking sound]. You can literally hear them on the sound track, the sound of them laughing like a bunch of geese just appeared from somewhere.

GA: Steven, of course, specializes in these really heavy movies like *Ocean's Eleven*, *Solaris*, and . . . was the mood quite intense on the set? Because when you watch this movie, it feels pretty claustrophobic and heavy and consistent.

SS: Yeah, we had people show up with smiles on their faces that left within five minutes.

GC: We also have to explain when you're on a set where Steven's directing, it's a really easygoing place. Not just on *Out of Sight* or *Ocean's*, even *Traffic*. It's difficult work, but there's a really professional air. It's fun. There's no yelling, there's nobody screaming, "Everybody, take your places!" So people come and visit, and it's a fun place to be. This one was very different: the day we wrapped, the two of us just walked out and sat on the back of this flatbed truck and had a beer. Usually there's a celebration, but we just sat there for an hour, and everybody was like, "Yeah, see you later."

ss: I don't know if I was just tired, because this was the seventh film that we'd done back-to-back with the same crew, pretty much. I don't know if it was the material. It was sort of agonizing because I wanted the film to be very simple in the way that it was done, and I found out the hard way that when you try to be simple, then each choice becomes incredibly important: where you put the camera, how you move the camera, how you pitch the scene. . . . With *Ocean's,* I'd be thinking, There are several ways that I could do this. But with this film, I would think that there's only one way, and it was incredibly difficult to figure out what this one way was. And there were many times on the set where Greg Jacobs, the assistant director who I've worked with since *King of the Hill,* would see that look on my face that I get like the floor has opened up in front of me, and he knows to start talking to me, when I'm sort of like somebody who's taken too much of a controlled substance, and he knows to start asking me questions to get me talking, to get me out of this terror, to keep me from telling him, "Call Fox, we're stopping. I'm stuck, I don't know what to do." And more than any other film I've made, we reshot material as we were shooting. It just seemed like each of the choices was critical. I learned from Richard Lester that as your career goes on, you learn more about how things can go wrong, but you never learn how things can go right. And it's really disorienting.

GA: What's it like directing your business partner? [To Clooney.] Do you feel that you can say, "No, I'm not doing this"?

GC: We're friends, we're partners, we share the same aesthetic, and we're trying to make the same kind of films. But he's a director, and directors are the captains of the ship, and it's your job as the lead actor to make sure that the rest of the cast understand that by doing whatever he says. It's never a problem with Steven. Everybody feels the same way. Having now directed something, I just can't imagine doing what he would do. He would go on to the set with a viewfinder, walk around and figure out how he should shoot it from how it should play. I planned everything, and I was really unfair to actors—"You gotta stand there, can't move." But Steven was like, "Well, let's see." And you would walk around, and he would find a way to cover it.

GA: So the first time you worked together was in *Out of Sight,* which came out at quite an interesting point in your career, Steven . . .

GC (laughing): In both our careers. *The Underneath* and *Batman and Robin*—we were on a roll.

GA: It wasn't even *The Underneath.* It was actually *Schizopolis* and *Gray's Anatomy,* which were smaller than *The Underneath* and very much underrated. You had turned your back on commercial films, and suddenly you were back with one of your most commercial films ever. Did you feel that was a real turning point for you, *Out of Sight*?

SS: Absolutely. It was a very conscious decision on my part to try and climb my way out of the art-house ghetto, which can be as much of a trap as making blockbuster films. And I was very aware that at that point in my career, half the business was off limits to me. And when I read the script, I thought, "I really know how to do this. I thought George, who was already attached, was the perfect person to do this part, and that it was a great opportunity for the both of us to show what we were capable of. As a result, I felt that I was under a tremendous amount of self-imposed pressure. I was very aware that if I didn't pull this off, that I would be in real trouble. Then you have to go on the set, block all that out, and shoot it as if you were shooting *Schizopolis,* and you're just going off what you think's the best idea in the moment, which is just like a kind of trick in the mind. But when the alarm clock went off in the morning, my stomach would lurch. But it was a very, very important film for me, personally and professionally.

GA: And yet it does bear some relationship to *Schizopolis* and everything you've done, from *Sex, Lies, and Videotape* up to *Solaris.* You have this fragmented narrative, and you're playing with film language, so it's not as if you were ever going into a different mode of filmmaking. You were just applying those sorts of things you do to a different sort of story.

SS: There were so many influences when I started watching films, whether it was Alain Resnais in *Out of Sight* or Nic Roeg. There was a scene in *Out of Sight* . . .

GA: Nic Roeg's here tonight.

GC: I ripped him off, too, and I want to apologize right now.

SS: . . . between George and Jennifer that's an actionable lift from *Don't Look Now*. And I've just always been fascinated by that form of storytelling. It's something that cinema does that I think truly re-creates our daily experience. I mean, let's say you're walking down the street and standing on the corner, and you think about something that somebody said to you yesterday, the meeting that you have to go to tomorrow, and you're watching the Don't Walk sign to see whether or not you can cross the street. And all these things are happening simultaneously in your head. Cinema re-creates that so well and so easily, so I've always gravitated to that, even when I was young and before I started thinking about films as anything other than entertainment.

GA (to Clooney): Steven has said he felt under pressure when he was making *Out of Sight*. What about you? You'd come out of a very successful television career, but your film career . . .

GC: Was not going well, is that what you're saying? [Laughter]

GA: Well, *Return of the Killer Tomatoes* was the high point . . .

GC: It *was* my high point, unfortunately, and still is.

GA: But it was as if this was the first film that seemed to know how to make use of you properly. I mean, the Tarantino film had been a lot of fun, but . . .

GC: Yeah, the Tarantino film was really important to me because . . . you needed to ride it when the show hit very early on, and the show was this juggernaut and arguably the most successful television show ever, and we were all on the tip of that thing and flying, and you could get quickly pigeonholed and not be able to do films. And so it was important that that first summer worked the way it did. There are things about it which were great and things which weren't, but it was important to me. See, the first thing about actors is, you're just trying to get a job; and you audition and audition, and you finally get them. And you still consider yourself an auditioning actor. I auditioned for *One Fine Day*; I wasn't offered that. So you're still in that, "Hey, I'm just trying to get a job" thing. Then you get to the point where if you decide to do it, then they'll make the film. That's a different kind of responsibility, and it usually takes a couple of films to catch up. And then you have to actually pay attention to the kind of films that you're making. [Laughter] Because as an actor, all you're looking for is a good part, and the problem is, you always think of the films as if Steven might be directing it, but the truth is, it's usually not Steven who's directing it. You got to think of things at their worst, not at their best. And *Out of Sight* was the first time where I had a say, and it was the first good screenplay that I'd read where I just went, "That's it." And even though it didn't do really well box office–wise—we sort of tanked again—it was a really good film. And I realized from that point on that it was strictly screenplay first. And then it becomes easier, because once you eliminate the idea of doing a vehicle . . . believe me, there's nobody who's encouraging us to make these films, not agents, not . . . we're not getting paid for these things, and it's not like we're going to make a mint. So there's nobody out there saying, "Here, go do this." So it has to be a sort of drive of your own to hammer this through, and it comes down to if you're willing to do it or not. Yeah, *Out of Sight* changed my career.

GA: Was it during the making of that film that you decided to form this company together?

SS: No, that came a little later. [To Clooney.] You'd had a partner and a company already.

GC: Yeah, we were developing about thirty-five projects. It was one of those things where Warner Brothers goes, "Hey, we'll give you this production deal, and it's already got a producer attached to it," and they put you together. It's literally like that, sort of Jerry Bruckheimer world, which works for him, but it doesn't work for the rest of the world. So he goes, "Okay, this one's called *Designated Survivor.* Everybody in the Senate is killed except for the one guy who's designated to go down into the basement of the White House for when the bomb goes off, and now he's president. And he's an action hero, too." [Laughter.] And I was busy working, you know. When you're shooting an hour TV series, you're busy. And I did seven films during that period. Very busy. So that was what was going on, and then I'd see my name in the trades attached to some project, and I'd think, "What the fuck am I doing, what is that?" And it's embarrassing. So when the deal came up, I was like, "Am I going to do this or not?" I don't want a vanity deal. Development for an actor who's famous means that they're going to try and pitch you the same project you've been successful in. "Okay, so in this one, you're like a bat and you're a man, and you're in rubber. And then, there's like a love interest." [Laughter.] And that doesn't work. So you try to do something different, try to make films that we like. [To Soderbergh.] You'd just finished *The Limey,* and we thought, Let's just go and do this.

ss: Yes, we share a similar taste and similar thoughts and a similar attitude to the business, and we thought we could get more accomplished working together rather than working on our own. And it's a director-driven company.

GA: Well, it's really paid off. *Insomnia*; next Friday we're seeing *Far from Heaven*, with Todd Haynes. And after that, we're screening *Confessions of a Dangerous Mind*.

GC: Yeah, that's fine.

ss: I didn't see it.

GC: You should see it.

ss: Really?

GC: Yeah, it's fantastic.

GA: Who gets to make the decisions about which films you make?

ss: We just have one rule, which is we both have to be jumping up and down and excited about it. And that's really the only rule, and so far it's worked. If there's any sort of hesitation on the part of either one of us, then we'll just let it go. We don't know how else to do it. The good news is that George and I are not producers by day, so as a result, we got paid on *Insomnia,* and we rolled the money into *Welcome to Collinwood.* So we don't have to collect a fee to keep the company going, so we're able to choose the projects that we're interested in. And in the case of *Insomnia,* Warner Brothers had their standard list of A-directors that they were going down. I'd heard that Chris Nolan, who I'd met, really wanted to make this but couldn't get in the door at Warners. And *Memento* hadn't come out, so our job was to slam Chris down Warner Brothers' throat and say, "This guy has a really interesting take on this material, this is the way you should go." And they agreed and said, "Why don't you guys just sort of be there with him?" He's very capable and certainly didn't need our help, except in cases like he wanted Wally Pfister for his D.P., and he wanted Dody Dorn as editor. Warners was initially thinking, "No, we want you to have a superstar cameraman and editor," and that was an instance where we come in and go, "No, he's got to have the people he's comfortable with." And that's our job, to protect him.

GC: We get things like final cut, and we give it back to the director. Because the thing is, you still need a point of view. And that's the problem that's happening with films. A million different people get involved in it, and they test the shit out of it, and then suddenly you go, "Wow, you've knocked off every edge to this thing." So our job is to protect the directors so they can make the films they want. So when it works, it works great. And we're like a tenth the cost of any of the production companies at Warner Brothers, because we set it up. And we've done five films in the past year, and none of the others did it because we were sort of able to say, "Look, it's not going to be as expensive, but it's not going to make as much money, probably."

GA: It's interesting, talking about helping people get the D.P. and editor they want. You seem to be working with Peter Andrews quite a lot on cinematography, and Mary Ann Bernard, I think, the editor. Can you talk a little bit about that? [To audience.] They're both Steven. How'd they get their names? Especially Mary Ann . . .

SS: Peter Andrews is my father's first two names. He was the one who gave me the cinema bug. He died very suddenly before *Out of Sight* was finished, so he's missed this whole run. And so, it was just a way to kind of pay tribute to him. Mary Ann Bernard is my mother's maiden name, and I realized late in life, because I was closer to my father, that I got a lot from my mother. She's a very nonlinear personality. And when I was growing up, I didn't know what to make of it and just found it kind of strange. My father was a much more linear personality, much more practical-minded, and I realized when I went through that *Schizopolis/Gray's Anatomy* phase that led to this group of films that there were many aspects to my mother's personality that were very much a part of me and should be amplified and explored. She's someone you could never imagine holding a nine-to-five job. She was interested in things like parapsychology and psychic surgery at a time when this was not cool. It was not on television—this was late sixties, early seventies, wife of a college professor at the University of Virginia. She was considered a kook. But she didn't care what other people thought, and she just went on her own path. And I realized that I got a lot from her, that I felt the same way about my work. If you're sitting around thinking what other people think about your work, you'll just become paralyzed.

GA: So you got the practical cinematographer and the nonlinear editor, which pretty much sums it up. But why are you so keen to do your own cinematography and editing when you're also producing, directing, and writing?

SS: I do my own driving, too.

GC: He's a control freak.

SS: No. You think? Actually, I don't really know. It's just a way to be as intimate with the film as possible. That's how I started, when I made short films, and it's a way to return to that sensation you had when you began, of making the film with your own hands. And it's a trade-off. I'm not world-class cinematographer, but the momentum and the closeness to the actors . . . I'm so close to them that I can just whisper to them while we're in the middle of a take. I remember Natascha [McElhone] made a comment that she felt in the scenes that we were doing together that she was doing it with George and with another performer because I was so close, and there was no one else around.

GC: We did scenes where there was not even a focus puller. It was literally just the three of us in a room. As an actor, that's a great thing, because when the director is looking at you through the eyepiece, you know that he's not kind of trying to discern what you're doing from some other weird image; he's really just right there. Steven could just look up from the camera and give me a look, and I would know what to do.

GA: This is quite different from the previous film, *Ocean's Eleven*, isn't it? Big cast and certainly couldn't be described as intimate. It's a lot of fun to watch. Was it as fun to make?

GC [laughing]: It was, for all the actors. It was the easiest shoot ever for any actor, and we all knew it when we were doing it. We were like, It's never going to be better than this. He was in hell, because it was a really complicated film to put together. We were like, we're in Las Vegas, we go to work at one in the afternoon, and we gotta be done by six at night. . . . Steven was editing all night.

SS: Yeah, I made it harder than it needed to be, because of this desire to get the actors in a room and see what evolves instead of trying to nail them down to some predetermined visual plan. The problem was, I had a movie that I felt demanded a fairly elaborate visual scheme, and I was interested in setting up these visual patterns in terms of movements that were very layered and interconnected. There are very few repeated shots in the film. But we were shooting it out of sequence, and I was making it up as I went. So it was very stressful. And it was a type of filmmaking that I hadn't really employed before, and that's why it was interesting to me. There are certain directors—Spielberg, David Fincher, John McTiernan—who sort of see things in three dimensions, and I was watching their films and sort of breaking them down to see how they laid sequences out, and how they paid attention to things like lens length, where the eyelines were, when the camera moved, how they cut, how they led your eye from one part of the frame to another. So I was trying to break all that down and watch how they worked and re-create it in ten minutes based on a rehearsal I'd just seen. So it was kind of stressful, but I didn't know how else to do it, and the only joy came when we put it together. We showed it to Warner Brothers seven days after we wrapped, and it was basically the film that was released. There was only one way to put it together, and I learned a lot, but my only moment of joy came during that week with [the editor] Stephen Mirrione, when we sort of polished the movie and showed it to the studio.

GA: Would you say that you like to set yourself challenges? You were talking about *Out of Sight* as a moment of pressure for you when you wanted to change your role in the industry; *Solaris* being a difficult film in some respects, and *Ocean's* being another challenge.

SS: Well, I think a part of you has to be scared. It keeps you alert. Otherwise, you become complacent. So absolutely, I'm purposefully going after things and doing things that I'm not sure if it's going to come off or not. Certainly *Full Frontal* was one of those. That was pure experimentation. That's the kind of film that you make going in where you know that a lot of people are not going to like it because it's an exploration of the contract that exists between the filmmaker and the audience and what happens when you violate that contract. But I felt after *Ocean's Eleven,* I need to do something like this, I need to go way over in the other direction or I run the risk of falling into a carved path that everybody's pushing you towards.

"Steven Soderbergh Starts a Revolution,"

(By David Sterritt. *Moviemaker*, Winter 2009)

In the two decades since *Sex, Lies, and Videotape* made him a superstar auteur, Steven Soderbergh has rarely lost a chance to defy expectations. He mastered crime comedy in *Out of Sight* and the *Ocean's* trilogy; he experimented with style in *Traffic, Full Frontal,* and *The Good Ger-*

man; he remade a Soviet classic, pioneered new distribution methods, and more. But the epic *Che*, about the Marxist radical Ernesto "Che" Guevara, is a daring project even for him—a four-hour-plus epic dealing with a violent revolutionary whose name still arouses strong passions, pro and con. Written by Peter Buchman and Benjamin A. van der Veen, who based the screenplay on Guevara's own writings, the film stars Benicio Del Toro and features a first-rate supporting cast, including Catalina Sandino Moreno, Julia Ormond, Demián Bichir, Lou Diamond Phillips, Franka Potente, Rodrigo Santoro, and many more.

Guevara was a multifaceted figure. Born and raised in Argentina, he became a medical doctor there, worked in Peru at a leper colony, joined the Cuban Revolution after meeting Fidel Castro in 1955, and led the revolutionary forces to victory in 1958. After filling major positions in Castro's government for several years, he clandestinely left Cuba for the Congo in 1965, then went the following year to Bolivia, where he hoped to spark an insurrection that would sweep throughout Latin America, but failed in the attempt and lost his life in the process.

Soderbergh originally wanted *Che* to focus entirely on the Bolivian campaign. Fund-raising went slowly, however, and he eventually handed the reins to Terrence Malick, who had been in Bolivia when Guevara was killed. Two years later, Malick stepped out to make *The New World*, and Soderbergh jumped back in, now wanting to include a large amount of material about the Cuban Revolution, which was shoehorned into an increasingly long screenplay with multiple timelines. To make things more manageable, Soderbergh decided to divide it between two movies, even though this meant rewriting distribution deals all over the planet. The chronological jumps survive to some extent in part 1, *The Argentine*, which leapfrogs among different events from 1955 to 1964. Part 2, *Guerrilla*, is a more linear chronicle of the Bolivian campaign and Guevara's downfall at enemy hands.

I first interviewed Soderbergh when he released his second feature, *Kafka*, in 1991, and I spoke with him again ten years later as chairman of the New York Film Critics Circle, when the three top awards—Best Picture and Best Director for Steven, Best Supporting Actor for Del Toro—went to *Traffic*, his 2000 tour de force. He was as candid and articulate as ever when we talked about *Che*.

DAVID STERRITT: This project is unusual, to say the least. How did it get started?

STEVEN SODERBERGH: It wasn't something I ever would have come up with on my own. It was during *Traffic* that [the producer] Laura Bickford and Benicio started talking to me about it, and I said yes without giving it a lot of thought. I didn't know that much about Che when we had the conversation, but I had an inkling it was going to be really tricky.

DS: Why did you say yes when you didn't know much about what you were getting into?

SS: I knew that if I don't say yes to things like this—having an opportunity to learn about a fascinating subject, knowing the guy who should be playing the part—then I'm kind of a poser. This is the kind of thing I *should* be doing.

DS: I imagine the logistics were difficult to put in place.

SS: The schedule and money were so tight that if I hadn't made all the films I did in the interim, including the *Ocean's* films, I don't think I would have been able to pull it off with the resources we had. . . . It was one of those projects that push everyone very hard, and you need fortitude and experience to get through it without freaking out. . . . But part of the game is to see if you can do it with what you have. I was working with the same team [as before], and everything we'd done since *Traffic* came into play somehow—everything from how to set up shots that you'd enhance later through visual effects to shooting sequences where guns and bombs are going off. As slow and frustrating as [developing the project] was at times, in a weird sort of way that turned out to be a good thing.

DS: What kind of research did you do?

SS: I read everything that was available, which is a lot, and we had access to almost everyone alive who knew Che well. Some of the things I learned that really stuck with me are details about the Cuban Revolution. Like a lot of people, I thought it was just Fidel, and I had no idea there were all these other factions trying to do something similar, and that there were real issues about how to coordinate these under the Fidel umbrella. I desperately wanted that in the film because it was part of how Che was educated. . . . He wasn't a compromiser, and it required him to adopt a different mindset than the warrior mentality he came in with.

DS: How did the large amount of facts and reportage and interviews you gathered affect the overall structure of the film? I'm particularly thinking of the complex time structure in part 1 and the more straightforward storytelling in part 2.

SS: I talked to the interpreter who was with Che for the whole week he was in New York to speak at the United Nations [in 1964], and that's when the idea of contrasting [the U.N. episode] with the Cuban campaign came into focus. I liked the idea of showing him at the absolute apex of his fame and notoriety, and juxtaposing that with him having an asthma attack in the jungle—sick and lost and still only a medic, not "Che" yet. With the Bolivia part, I knew absolutely nothing about how he died, but three of the people who were with him in Bolivia are still around, and we talked to them, and that was really intense. So we came back with trunks full of really interesting information, and in that situation you have to decide what your filter will be. My filter was that I'm interested in detail, in one-on-one encounters, in situations where Che was teaching the others—not teaching a large-scale macro-ideology but a day-to-day practical lesson in how to be a guerrilla fighter. So, as often happens, I started by defining the movie in terms of what I didn't want it to be.

DS: Something we have to discuss is the stance you take regarding Che and violence. He's still hugely controversial, and the film seems to take a neutral approach toward him. Psychologically, for instance, it doesn't speculate on what might have driven him to become a violent revolutionary.

SS: I decided that I'm going to show you a bunch of stuff that he did, and you can determine for yourself how you come down on that. For people who are very anti-Che, we conveniently, in their minds, skipped the period right after the revolution when . . . he committed the acts [of violence and oppression] that really get people pissed off. But that wasn't part of his life that I was interested in portraying. I basically wanted to make two war movies. . . . I'm not Latino, and I don't have any interest in building him up or tearing him down, because it's not an emotional investment for me.

DS: But haven't you left yourself open to attack by leaving out actions that turned a lot of people against him?

SS: Those things are addressed in the film, based on my research, in a [proportion] that's appropriate [to the film as a whole]. . . . We do see him supervise the executions of deserters, and he does say at the U.N. that "we kill people, and we're gonna keep on killing them." But every regime, whether it's us or any other country, acts in an excessive manner when it feels threatened. So if you want to talk about [the revolutionary tribunals and executions at the Havana fortress called] La Cabaña, then let's talk about the firebombing of Japan and the second atomic bomb. Regimes do these things out of an emotional need to solidify a position . . . because they don't want people coming up behind them and saying, "The enemy is back! Why didn't you solve this!" So if you want to point fingers, there are plenty of places to point, in every direction.

DS: The fact remains that Guevara was a violent revolutionary who killed an awful lot of people. Isn't anyone who comes within thinking distance of that obligated to take a stand on it?

SS: Absolutely, yeah. I look at him and say he was a guy who picked up a gun, which isn't something we often encourage people to do. But you have to consider the context in which he lived, the conditions in that part of the world, at that point in time, when every country in the Caribbean and Latin America was run by a leader in the pocket of the United States, and they were being used as machines to make money for the U.S. That's not the case now, partially because of the events of fifty years ago. So when a young guy who's well-read and well-educated becomes radicalized and decides to pick up a gun and join a bunch of other guys who've picked up guns—that was a much more logical and understandable decision fifty years ago in that part of the world. And the other thing you have to consider, whether you like him or not, is that he decided to put his life on the line for people he didn't know and had never met, and he did it at least three times that we're aware of: in Cuba, in the Congo, and in Bolivia. The second two times were after he'd gotten married and set up a family, and he could have ridden out the rest of his years in Cuba in a pretty comfortable fashion. But he decided to drop everything and go back and be that guy in the jungle again. He never made a nickel, [and] he wasn't interested in power. He made no bones about the fact that he was ready and willing to kill or be killed in support of his ideas. The way he died was very consistent with the way he lived, and he was never hesitant about that.

DS: Do you see *Che* as a political film?

ss: I don't think anybody walks out of a movie with their mind changed. . . . But if you make any film that accurately portrays the world as it is, that portrays people's lives the way they actually are, by definition that's a political film.

ds: What messages would you like audiences to take away from *Che*?

ss: During the shoot I referred to Che's struggle as an "analog revolution." We're not in that world anymore. But what I hope people will think about is the issue of how engaged *our* lives are, personally or locally or globally. I think Che's absolute, total commitment to engaging is really compelling to consider. The only thing I feel that passionate about, although I guess it's pretty small, is my work. In every other area, forget it. So my way to get through [telling Guevara's story] without going insane was to view it as an analogy for making art. This is my version of getting out from behind the desk and going back into the jungle. You have to keep finding things that put you back into that place of fear.

Feature Films

Sex, Lies, and Videotape (1989)
Producer: Outlaw Productions
Distributor: Miramax
Director: Steven Soderbergh
Screenplay: Steven Soderbergh
Photography: Walt Lloyd
Editor: Steven Soderbergh
Music: Cliff Martinez
Cast: James Spader (Graham Dalton), Andie MacDowell (Ann Mullany),
    Peter Gallagher (John Mullany), Laura San Giacomo (Cynthia Bishop),
    Ron Vawter (Therapist), Steven Brill (Barfly), Earl T. Taylor (Landlord),
    David Foil (John's Colleague)
Color
100 min.

Kafka (1991)
Producer: Baltimore Pictures
Distributor: Miramax
Director: Steven Soderbergh
Screenplay: Lem Dobbs
Photography: Walt Lloyd
Editor: Steven Soderbergh
Music: Cliff Martinez
Cast: Jeremy Irons (Kafka), Theresa Russell (Gabriela), Joel Gray (Burgel),
    Ian Holm (Dr. Murnau), Jeroen Krabbé (Bizzlebek), Armin Mueller-Stahl
    (Grubach), Alec Guiness (The Chief Clerk), David Jensen (Laughing Man)
Black and white, Color
98 min.

King of the Hill (1993)
Producer: Bona Fide Productions
Distributor: Gramercy Pictures
Director: Steven Soderbergh
Screenplay: Steven Soderbergh
Photography: Elliot Davis
Editor: Steven Soderbergh
Music: Cliff Martinez
Cast: Jesse Bradford (Aaron Kurlander), Jeroen Krabbé (Kurlander), Lisa
    Eichorn (Mrs. Kurlander), Karen Allen (Miss Mathey), Spalding Gray (Mr.
    Mungo), Elizabeth McGovern (Lydia), John Durbin (Mr. Sandoz), Joe
    Chrest (Ben), Cameron Boyd (Sullivan Kurlander), Adrien Brody (Lester),
    John McConnell (Officer Burns)
Color
102 min.

The Underneath (1995)
Producer: Universal Pictures
Distributor: Gramercy Pictures
Director: Steven Soderbergh
Screenplay: Steven Soderbergh (as Sam Lowry)
Photography: Elliot Davis
Editor: Stan Salfas
Music: Cliff Martinez
Cast: Peter Gallagher (Michael Chambers), Alison Elliot (Rachel), Elisabeth
    Shue (Susan), Joe Don Baker (Clay Hinkle), Paul Dooley (Ed), William
    Fichtner (Tommy Dundee), Adam Trese (David Chambers), Anjanette
    Comer (Mrs. Chambers), Shelley Duvall (Nurse)
Color
99 min.

Gray's Anatomy (1996)
Producers: Independent Film Channel, BBC
Distributor: Northern Arts Entertainment
Director: Steven Soderbergh
Screenplay: Spalding Gray
Photography: Elliot Davis
Editor: Susan Littenberg
Music: Cliff Martinez
Cast: Spalding Gray
Color
80 min.

Schizopolis (1996)
Producer: .406 Production
Distributor: Northern Arts Entertainment
Director: Steven Soderbergh
Screenplay: Steven Soderbergh
Photography: Steven Soderbergh
Editor: Sarah Flack
Music: Cliff Martinez
Cast: Steven Soderbergh (Fletcher Munson/Dr. Jeffrey Korchek), Betsy
    Brantley (Mrs. Munson), David Jensen (Elmo Oxygen)
Color
96 min.

Out of Sight (1998)
Producer: Jersey Films
Distributor: Universal Pictures
Director: Steven Soderbergh
Screenplay: Scott Frank
Photography: Elliot Davis
Editor: Anne Coates
Music: David Holmes
Cast: George Clooney (Jack Foley), Jennifer Lopez (Karen Sisco), Ving
    Rhames (Buddy), Dennis Farina (Marshall Sisco), Don Cheadle (Maurice
    "Snoopy" Miller), Isaiah Washington (Kenneth), Steve Zahn (Glen
    Michaels), Catherine Keener (Adele), Luis Guzman (Chino), Albert
    Brooks (Richard Ripley), Keith Loneker (White Boy Bob)
Color
123 min.

The Limey (1999)
Producer: Artisan Entertainment
Director: Steven Soderbergh
Screenplay: Lem Dobbs
Photography: Ed Lachman
Editor: Sarah Flack
Music: Cliff Martinez
Cast: Terence Stamp (Wilson), Peter Fonda (Terry Valentine), Leslie Ann
    Warren (Elaine), Luis Guzman (Eduardo Roel), Barry Newman (Jim
    Avery), Nicky Katt (Stacey), Melissa George (Jenny), Bill Duke (DEA
    Agent), William Lucking (Warehouse Foreman)
Color
89 min.

Erin Brockovich (2000)
Producer: Jersey Films
Distributor: Universal
Director: Steven Soderbergh
Screenplay: Susannah Grant
Photography: Ed Lachman
Editor: Anne Coates
Music: Cliff Martinez
Cast: Julia Roberts (Erin Brockovich), Aaron Eckhart (George), Albert
    Finney (Ed Masry), Peter Coyote (Kurt Potter)
Color
130 min.

Traffic (2000)
Producer: USA Films
Distributor: Northern Arts Entertainment
Director: Steven Soderbergh
Screenplay: Stephen Gaghan
Photography: Steven Soderbergh
Editor: Stephen Mirrione
Music: Cliff Martinez
Cast: Michael Douglas (Robert Wakefield), Catherine Zeta-Jones (Helena
    Ayala), Benecio Del Toro (Javier Rodriguez), Don Cheadle (Montel
    Gordon), Luis Guzman (Ray Castro), Dennis Quaid (Arnie Metzer), Amy
    Irving (Barbara Wakefield), Miguel Ferrer (Eduardo Ruiz), Topher Grace
    (Seth Abrahms), Erika Christensen (Catherine Wakefield), Clifton Collins
    (Francisco Flores), Jacob Vargas (Manolo), Tomas Milian (Gen. Salazar)
Color
147 min.

Ocean's Eleven (2001)
Producer: Jerry Weintraub Productions
Distributor: Warner Bros.
Director: Steven Soderbergh
Screenplay: Ted Griffin
Photography: Steven Soderbergh (as Peter Andrews)
Editor: Stephen Mirrione
Music: David Holmes
Cast: George Clooney (Danny Ocean), Brad Pitt (Rusty Ryan), Bernie Mac
    (Frank Catton), Elliot Gould (Reuben Tishkoff), Don Cheadle (Basher
    Tarr), Casey Affleck (Virgil Malloy), Scott Caan (Turk Malloy), Matt
    Damon (Linus Caldwell), Carl Reiner (Saul Bloom), Eddie Jemison

(Livingston Dell), Andy Garcia (Terry Benedict), Julia Roberts (Tess Ocean), Shaobo Qin (Yao)
Color
116 min.

Full Frontal (2002)
Producer and distributor: Miramax Films
Director: Steven Soderbergh
Screenplay: Coleman Hough
Photography: Steven Soderbergh
Editor: Stephen Mirrione
Music: David Holmes
Cast: David Duchovny (Gus), Nicky Katt (Hitler), Catherine Keener (Lee), Mary McCormack (Linda), David Hyde Pierce (Carl), Blair Underwood (Nicholas/Calvin), Enrico Colantoni (Artie), Julia Roberts (Catherine/ Francesca)
Color
101 min.

Solaris (2002)
Producer and distributor: Twentieth Century-Fox
Director: Steven Soderbergh
Screenplay: Steven Soderbergh
Photography: Steven Soderbergh (as Peter Andrews)
Editor: Steven Soderbergh (as Mary Ann Bernard)
Music: Cliff Martinez
Cast: George Clooney (Chris Kelvin), Natascha McElhone (Rheya), Viola Davis (Gordon), Jeremy Davis (Snow), Ulrich Tukur (Gibarian)
Color
99 min.

Ocean's Twelve (2004)
Producer and distributor: Warner Bros.
Director: Steven Soderbergh
Screenplay: George Nolfi
Photography: Steven Soderbergh (as Peter Andrews)
Editor: Stephen Mirrione
Music: David Holmes
Cast: George Clooney (Danny Ocean), Brad Pitt (Rusty Ryan), Bernie Mac (Frank Catton), Elliot Gould (Reuben Tishkoff), Don Cheadle (Basher Tarr), Casey Affleck (Virgil Malloy), Scott Caan (Turk Malloy), Matt Damon (Linus Caldwell), Carl Reiner (Saul Bloom), Eddie Jemison

(Livingston Dell), Andy Garcia (Terry Benedict), Julia Roberts (Tess Ocean), Shaobo Qin (Yao), Catherine Zeta-Jones (Isabel Lahiri), Bruce Willis (Himself), Vincent Cassell (Toulour)
Color
125 min.

Bubble (2005)
Producer: Gregory Jacobs
Distributor: Magnolia Pictures
Director: Steven Soderbergh
Screenplay: Coleman Hough
Photography: Steven Soderbergh (as Peter Andrews)
Editor: Steven Soderbergh (as Mary Ann Bernard)
Music: Robert Pollard
Cast: Debbie Doebereiner (Martha), Misty Wilkins (Rose), Decker Moody (Detective Don Taylor), Dustin Ashley (Kyle)
Color
73 min.

The Good German (2006)
Producer and distributor: Warner Bros.
Director: Steven Soderbergh
Photography: Steven Soderbergh (as Peter Andrews)
Editor: Steven Soderbergh (as Mary Ann Bernard)
Music: Thomas Newman
Cast: Jack Thompson (Congressman Breimer), George Clooney (Jake Geismer), Cate Blanchett (Lena Brandt), Tobey Maguire (Tully), Christian Oliver (Emil Brandt), Beau Bridges (Colonel Muller)
Black and White
105 min.

Ocean's Thirteen (2007)
Producer and distributor: Warner Bros.
Director: Steven Soderbergh
Screenplay: George Nolfi
Photography: Steven Soderbergh
Editor: Stephen Mirrione
Music: David Holmes
Cast: George Clooney (Danny Ocean), Brad Pitt (Rusty Ryan), Bernie Mac (Frank Catton), Elliot Gould (Reuben Tishkoff), Don Cheadle (Basher Tarr), Casey Affleck (Virgil Malloy), Scott Caan (Turk Malloy), Matt Damon (Linus Caldwell), Carl Reiner (Saul Bloom), Eddie Jemison (Livingston Dell), Andy Garcia (Terry Benedict), Al Pacino (Willy Bank),

Shaobo Qin (Yao), Vincent Cassel (Toulour), Ellen Barkin (Abigail
Sponder), Eddie Izzard (Roman Nagel)
Color
122 min.

Che (Part 1: *The Argentine*) (2008)
Producers: Estudios Picasso, Wild Bunch, Section Eight
Distributor: IFC Films
Director: Steven Soderbergh
Screenplay: Peter Buchman
Photography: Steven Soderbergh (as Peter Andrews)
Editor: Pablo Zumarraga
Music: Alberto Iglesias
Cast: Benicio Del Toro (Ernesto "Che" Guevara), Franka Potente (Tania),
Demián Bichir (Fidel Castro), Rodrigo Santoro (Raul Castro), Julia
Ormond (Lisa Howard), Lou Diamond Phillips (Mario Monje)
Color
129 min.

Che (Part 2: *Guerilla*) (2008)
Producers: Estudios Picasso,Wild Bunch, Section Eight
Distributor: IFC Films
Director: Steven Soderbergh
Screenplay: Peter Buchman
Photography: Steven Soderbergh (as Peter Andrews)
Editor: Pablo Zumarraga
Music: Alberto Iglesias
Cast: Benicio Del Toro (Ernesto "Che" Guevara), Franka Potente (Tania),
Demián Bichir (Fidel Castro), Rodrigo Santoro (Raul Castro), Santiago
Cabrera (Camilo Cienfuegos), Catalina Sandido Moreno (Aleida March)
Color
129 min.

The Informant! (2009)
Producers: Warner Bros., Section Eight
Distributor: Warner Bros.
Director: Steven Soderbergh
Screenplay: Scott Burns, Kurt Eichenwald
Photography: Steven Soderbergh (as Peter Andrews)
Editor: Stephen Mirrione
Music: Marvin Hamlisch
Cast: Matt Damon (Mark Whitacre), Lucas McHugh Carroll (Alexander
Whitacre), Eddie Jemison (Kirk Schmidt), Rusty Schwimmer (Liz Taylor),

Tom Papa (Mick Andreas), Rick Overton (Terry Wilson), Melanie Lynskey (Ginger Whitacre), Thomas F. Wilson (Mark Cheviron), Scott Bakula (Brian Shepard), John McHale (Robert Herndon), Patton Oswalt (Ed Herbst), Scott Adsit (Sid Hulse), Clancy Brown (Aubrey Daniel), Tony Hale (James Epstein), Andrew Daly (Marty Allison), Frank Welker (Mark Whitacre's Father), Dick Smothers (Judge Harold Baker), Tom Smothers (Dwayne Andreas), Richard Steven Horvitz (Bob Zaiderman)
Color
108 min.

The Girlfriend Experience (2009)
Producers: Mark Cuban, Gregory Jacobs, Todd Wagner
Director: Steven Soderbergh
Screenplay: David Levien and Brian Koppelman
Photography: Steven Soderbergh (as Peter Andrews)
Editor: Steven Soderbergh
Music: Ross Godfrey
Cast: Sasha Grey (Chelsea), Chris Santos (Chris), Phillip Eytan (Phillip), Mark Jacobson (Interviewer)
Color
77 min.

TV Series

K Street (2003)
Producer: Section Eight
Distributor: HBO
Screenplay: Henry Bean
Photography: Steven Soderbergh
Editor: Steven Soderbergh
Cast: Mary McCormack (Maggie), John Slattery (Tommy Flannegan), Mary Matalin (Herself), James Carville (Himself), Roger G. Smith (Francisco), Jennice Fuentes (Ana)
Color
10 episodes (30 min. each)

Bibliography |

Akass, Kim, and Janet McCabe. "Adieu to *The Sopranos*: What Next for HBO?" *FlowTV* 6 (May 18, 2007); accessed July 15, 2010. http://flowtv.org/2007/05/adieu-to-the-sopranos-what-next-for-hbo/.

Anderson, John. "Down South, Singing the Indie Blues." *New York Times,* December 2, 2007, 14.

———. "Of Crime and Perception at Abu Ghraib." *New York Times,* April 20, 2008, 15.

Anderson, John Lee. *Che Guevara: A Revolutionary Life.* New York: Grove Press, 1997.

Arenas, Alberto. "In Defense of Good Work: Jobs, Violence, and the Ethical Dimension." *Social Justice* 30.3 (2000): 94–107.

Atkinson, Michael. Rev. of *The Informant! Sight and Sound* (December 2009); accessed July 19, 2010. http://www.bfi.org.uk/sightandsound/review/5229/.

Bankston, Douglas. "Smooth Operators: *Ocean's Eleven*." *American Cinematographer* (January 2002); accessed July 19, 2010. www.stevensoderbergh.net/articles/2002/cinematographer.php.

Bart, Peter, and Michael Fleming. "Sony Scraps Soderbergh's *Moneyball*." *Variety,* June 21, 2009; accessed July 8, 2010. www.variety.com/article/VR1118005208.html?categoryid=13&cs=1.

Biskind, Peter. *Down and Dirty Pictures: Miramax, Sundance, and the Rise of Independent Film.* New York: Simon and Schuster, 2004.

Blankstein, Andrew. "Chromium 6 Released into L.A. River for Years." *Los Angeles Times,* October 30, 2000, A1.

Bordwell, David. "Art-Cinema Narration." In *Narration in the Fiction Film.* Madison: University of Wisconsin Press, 1985. 205–33.

———. "Authorship and Narration in Art Cinema." In *Film and Authorship.* Ed. Virgina Wright Wexman. New Brunswick, N.J.: Rutgers University Press, 2003. 42–49.

———. *The Way Hollywood Tells It: Story and Style in Modern Movies.* Los Angeles: University of California Press, 2006.

Bordwell, David, and Kristin Thompson. *Film Art: An Introduction.* 8th ed. New York: McGraw Hill, 2008.

Boyd, Todd. *The New HNIC: The Death of Civil Rights and the Reign of Hip Hop.* New York: New York University Press, 2002.

Bruce, Iris. "Kafka and Jewish Folklore." In *The Cambridge Companion to Kafka.* Ed. Julian Preece. Cambridge: Cambridge University Press, 2002. 150–68.

Brunsdon, Charlotte. *Screen Tastes: Soap Opera to Satellite Dishes.* London: Routledge, 1997.

Buscomb, Edward. "Ideas of Authorship." In *Theories of Authorship.* Ed. John Caughie. New York: Routledge, 2001. 22–34.

Caldwell, John. *Production Culture: Industrial Reflexivity and Critical Practice in Film and Television.* Durham, N.C.: Duke University Press, 2008.

Carroll, Noel. "The Future of Allusion: Hollywood in the Seventies (and Beyond)." In *Interpreting the Moving Image.* New York: Cambridge University Press, 1998. 240–64.

———. "The Specificity Thesis." In *Film Theory and Criticism: Introductory Readings.* 4th ed. Ed. Gerald Mast, Marshall Cohen, and Leo Braudy. New York: Oxford University Press, 1999. 322–28.

Cheshire, Godrey. "Star Gazing." *altweeklies.com*; accessed November 1, 2005. http://www.indyweek.com/durham/2001-12.051/movie.html.

Corrigan, Timothy. "Auteurs and the New Hollywood." In *The New American Cinema.* Ed. Jon Lewis. Durham, N.C.: Duke University Press, 1998. 38–63.

Dargis, Manohla. "A List, to Start the Conversation." *New York Times,* December 23, 2007, 14.

Denton, Sally, and Robert Morris. *The Money and the Power: The Making of Las Vegas and Its Hold on America.* New York: Knopf, 2001.

Dodd, Bill. "The Case for a Political Reading." In *The Cambridge Companion to Kafka.* Ed. Julian Preece. Cambridge: Cambridge University Press, 2002. 131–49.

Dyer, Richard. "Entertainment and Utopia." In *Movies and Methods.* Vol. 2. Ed. Bill Nichols. Los Angeles: University of California Press, 1985. 220–32.

Ebert, Roger. *Roger Ebert's Movie Home Companion.* Kansas City: Andrews and McNeel, 1992.

Epstein, David Robert. "Interview with Steven Soderbergh." *Suicide Girls.* January 22, 2006; accessed July 1, 2007. http://suicidegirls.com/interviews/Steven+Soderbergh/.

Faux, Jeff. "So Far from God, So Close to Wall St." *The Nation,* July 15, 2009; accessed October 1, 2010. http://www.thenation.com/article/so-far-god-so-close-wall-st.

Fuchs, Cynthia. Rev. of *The Good German. Pop Matters,* December 18, 2006; accessed July 9, 2010. http://www.popmatters.com/pm/review/the-good-german-2006/.

Garcia, Oskar. "U.S. Gambling Revenues Up 5.4 Percent to $34 Billion in 2007." *Forbes,* June 7, 2008; accessed June 7, 2008. http://www.forbes.com/feeds/ap/2008/05/14/ap5009845.html.

Garland, David. *The Culture of Control: Crime and Social Order in Contemporary Society.* Chicago: University of Chicago Press, 2001.

Garrett, Stephen. "Will *Che* Director Steven Soderbergh Retire in 2015? (Maybe.)" *Esquire,* January 23, 2009; accessed July 15, 2010. http://www.esquire.com/features/the-screen/steven-soderbergh-interview-0209.

Gilman, Sander. *Franz Kafka, the Jewish Patient.* New York: Routledge, 1995.

Grady, Pam. "A Talk with Steven Soderbergh: The Man behind *Erin Brockovich.*" *Reel.com* (February 2000); accessed May 28, 2008. http://www.stevensoderbergh.net/articles/2000/reel.php.

Gross, Terry. "Soderbergh's *Bubble* Changes the Rules." *Fresh Air.* National Public Radio, January 24, 2006; accessed July 19, 2010. www.npr.org/templates/story/story.php?storyId=5167394.

Hacker, Jacob S. *The Great Risk Shift: The Assault on American Jobs, Families, Health Care, and Retirement—and How You Can Fight Back.* New York: Oxford University Press, 2006.

Hirschberg, Lynn. "What Is an American Movie Now?" *New York Times,* November 14, 2004; accessed July 15, 2010. http://www.nytimes.com/2004/11/14/movies/14HOLLYWOOD.html.

Hoberman, J. "Crime Scenes." *Village Voice,* July 30, 2002; accessed July 15, 2010. http://www.villagevoice.com/2002-07–30/film/crime-scenes/.

Holmlund, Chris. "Postfeminism from A to G." *Cinema Journal* 44.2 (Winter 2005): 116–21.

Holson, Laura M. "Trying to Combine Art and Box Office in Hollywood." *New York Times,* January 17, 2005; accessed July 8, 2010. http://www.nytimes.com/2005/01/17/business/media/17clooney.html.

Hornaday, Ann. "'Bubble' Vision." *Washington Post,* January 22, 2006, N1.

Kaufman, Anthony. *Steven Soderbergh Interviews.* Jackson: University Press of Mississippi, 2002.

Kehr, Dave. "You Can Make 'em Like They Used To." *New York Times,* November 12, 2006, 1, 15.

King, Barry. "Articulating Stardom." In *Stardom: Industry of Desire.* Ed. Christine Gledhill. London: Routledge, 1991. 167–82.

King, Geoff. *American Independent Cinema.* Bloomington: Indiana University Press, 2005.

Kleinhans, Chuck. "Independent Features, Hopes and Dreams." In *The New American Cinema.* Ed. Jon Lewis. Durham, N.C.: Duke University Press, 1998. 307–27.

Kozloff, Sarah. *Overhearing Film Dialogue.* Los Angeles: University of California Press, 2000.

Lane, Anthony. "Che's Way." *New Yorker,* January 19, 2009, 72–74.

Lears, Jackson. *Something for Nothing: Luck in America.* New York: Viking, 2003.

Lehman, Peter, and William Luhr. *Thinking about Movies: Watching, Questioning, Enjoying.* 3d ed. Malden, Mass.: Blackwell, 2008.

Leitch, Thomas. "Twice-Told Tales: The Rhetoric of the Remake." *Literature/ Film Quarterly* 18.3 (1990): 138–49.

Levitt, Steven D. "Understanding Why Crime Fell in the 1990s: Four Factors That Explain the Decline and Six That Do Not." *Journal of Economic Perspectives* 18.1 (Winter 2004): 163–90.

Lim, Dennis. "Screenwriting Drafts of History." *New York Times,* January 4, 2009, 4.

Littleton, Cynthia. "DGA Makes Big Gains in New Media" *Variety,* January 26, 2008; accessed July 15, 2010. www.variety.com/article/VR1117979254.html.

Maltby, Richard. *Hollywood Cinema.* 2d ed. Malden, Mass.: Blackwell, 2003.

Marez, Curtis. *Drug Wars: The Political Economy of Narcotics.* Minneapolis: University of Minnesota Press, 2004.

McCarthy, Todd. Rev. of *Che. Variety,* May 21, 2008; accessed June 28, 2010. http:// www.variety.com/review/VE1117937244.html?categoryid=2863&cs=1.

———. Rev. of *Full Frontal. Variety,* July 25, 2002; accessed July 15, 2010. http:// www.variety.com/review/VE1117918279.html?categoryid=31&cs=1.

McGowan, Richard A. "Ethics of Gambling." *Boston Globe,* September 21, 2007; accessed October 19, 2010. http://www.boston.com/news/globe/editorial_ opinion/oped/articles/2007/09/21/ethics_of_gambling/.

McLean, Thomas. "Section Eight Goes Up in Smoke." *Variety,* October 12, 2006; accessed July 8, 2010. http://www.variety.com/article/VR1117951781 .html?categoryid=2294&cs=1.

Mizejewski, Linda. *Hardboiled and High Heeled: The Woman Detective in Popular Culture.* New York: Routledge, 2004.

Mohr, Ian. "Cuban Rhythm Shakes Up Films." *Variety,* May 4, 2007; accessed July 15, 2010. http://www.variety.com/article/VR1117964308 .html?categoryid=2520&cs=1.

Mouw, Ted. "Job Relocation and the Racial Gap in Unemployment in Detroit and Chicago, 1980–1990." *American Sociological Review* 65 (October 2000): 730–53.

Murray, Rebecca. "George Clooney Discusses *The Good German.*" *About.com*; accessed September 14, 2010. http://movies.about.com/od/thegoodgerman/a/ germangc120106.htm.

Naremore, James. "Authorship and the Cultural Politics of Film Criticism." *Film Quarterly* 44.1 (Fall 1990): 14–22.

———. *More Than Night: Film Noir in Its Contexts.* Los Angeles: University of California Press, 1998.

Newman, Thomas Z. "Indie Culture: In Pursuit of the Authentic Autonomous Alternative." *Cinema Journal* 48.3 (Spring 2009): 16–34.

Ocean's Eleven. Dir. Steven Soderbergh. DVD. Commentary by Steven Soderbergh. Warner Bros., 2001.

Out of Sight. Dir. Steven Soderbergh. DVD. Commentary by Steven Soderbergh. Universal, 1998.

Pham, Alex. "Sony Sales Slide 20 Percent as Global Economy Erodes." *Los Angeles Times,* October 30, 2009; accessed October 9, 2010. http://latimesblogs .latimes.com/technology/2009/10/sony-second-quarter-2010-earnings.html.

Prince, Stephen. *Savage Cinema: Sam Peckinpah and the Rise of Ultraviolent Movies.* Austin: University of Texas Press, 1998.

———. *Screening Violence.* Piscataway, N.J.: Rutgers University Press, 2000.

Rafter, Nicole. *Shots in the Mirror: Crime Films and Society.* Oxford: Oxford University Press, 2006.

Ray, Robert. *A Certain Tendency of the Hollywood Cinema, 1930–1980.* Princeton, N.J.: Princeton University Press, 1985.

Reed, Kimberly. "Steven Soderbergh's Return to Roots." *DV.com,* September 7, 2002; accessed July 15, 2010. http://www.dv.com/article/16630.

Ressner, Jeffrey. "*Che* Relevant to American Politics." *Politico,* December 12, 2008; accessed July 15, 2010. http://www.politico.com/news/stories/1208/16503 .html.

Roffman, Peter, and Jim Purdy. *The Hollywood Social Problem Film: Madness, Despair, and Politics from the Depression to the Fifties.* Bloomington: Indiana University Press, 1981.

Romney, Jonathan. "Future Soul." *Sight and Sound* 13.2 (February 2003): 14–18.

Rosenbaum, Jonathan. "In Space, No One Can Hear You Sweat." *Chicago Reader,* February 11, 2004; accessed July 8, 2010. http://www.chicagoreader .com/chicago/in-space-no-one-can-hear-you-sweat/Content?oid=910573.

Rosenstone, Robert. *Visions of the Past: The Challenge of Film to Our Idea of History.* Cambridge, Mass.: Harvard University Press, 1998.

Salamon, Julie. "Before Hollywood's *Traffic* Came the Elegant *Traffik.*" *New York Times,* July 6, 2001; accessed July 8, 2010. http://www.nytimes .com/2001/07/06/movies/tv-weekend-before-hollywood-s-traffic-came-the- elegant-traffik.html.

Scott, A. O. "'Tis Pity She's a Brand." Rev. of *The Girlfriend Experience. New York Times,* May 22, 2009; accessed June 28, 2010. http://movies.nytimes .com/2009/05/22/movies/22girl.html.

Sex, Lies, and Videotape. Dir. Steven Soderbergh. DVD. Commentary by Steven Soderbergh. Columbia/TriStar, 1989.

Silverman, Jason. "Soderbergh: Burn, Hollywood, Burn." *Wired,* May 3, 2006; accessed July 15, 2010. http://www.wired.com/culture/lifestyle/ news/2006/05/70795.

Smith, Gavin. "Hired Gun: Steven Soderbergh—Interview." *Film Comment* 37.1 (January 2001): 26–31.

Soderbergh, Steven. *Getting Away with It; Or, The Further Adventures of the Luckiest Bastard You Ever Saw.* London: Faber and Faber, 1999.

Solaris. Dir. Steven Soderbergh. DVD. Commentary by Steven Soderbergh. Twentieth-Century Fox, 2002.

Spada, James. *Julia: Her Life*. New York: St. Martin's, 2004.

Suber, Howard. "Why They Hate Our Movies." *Huffington Post,* September, 13, 2006; accessed July 19, 2010. http://www.huffingtonpost.com/howard-suber/why-they-hate-our-movies_b_29396.html.

Taubin, Amy. "Degraded Dupes Steven Soderbergh" *Sight and Sound* (March 2007); accessed June 28, 2010. http://www.bfi.org.uk/sightandsound/feature/49360.

———. "Fear of a Black Cinema." *Sight and Sound* (August 2002); accessed June 28, 2010. http://www.bfi.org.uk/sightandsound/feature/42.

———. "*K Street*: Washington Inside-Out." *Film Comment* online exclusive (2004); accessed February 27, 2006. http//www.filmlinc.com/fcm/online/kstreet.htm.

Taylor, Ella. "Lost and Found. The Human Souls of *Full Frontal* and *Group*." *L.A. Weekly,* July 31, 2002; accessed July 9, 2010. http://www.laweekly.com/2002-08-08/film-tv/lost-and-found/.

Tonguette, Peter. Rev. of *Full Frontal. Film Journal* 3 (2002); accessed July 19, 2010. http://www.thefilmjournal.com/issue3/fullfrontal2.html.

Toossi, Mitra. "Consumer Spending: An Engine of U.S. Job Growth." *Monthly Labor Review* 125.11 (November 2002): 12–22.

Wasser, Frederick. "Political Polarization and the New Hollywood Blockbuster." *FlowTV* 1 (October 22, 2004); accessed July 15, 2010. http://flowtv.org/2004/10/political-polarization-and-the-new-hollywood-blockbuster/.

———. *Veni, Vidi, Video: The Hollywood Empire and the VCR*. Austin: University of Texas Press, 2002.

Williams, David. "Mad-Dog Englishman." *American Cinematographer* 80.11 (November 1999): 54–65.

Wolff, Edward N. "Recent Trends in Living Standards in the United States." In *What Has Happened to the Quality of Life in the Advanced Industrialized Nations?* Ed. Edward N. Wolff. Northampton, Mass.: Edward Elgar, 2004. 3–26.

Wyatt, Justin. "The Formation of the 'Major Independent': Miramax, New Line, and the New Hollywood." In *Contemporary Hollywood Cinema*. Ed. Steven Neale and Murray Smith. New York: Routledge, 1998. 74–90.

Zeitchik, Steven. "Download Demand: Netflix Plans to Expand Online Efforts." *Variety,* January 24, 2006; accessed July 15, 2010. http://www.variety.com/article/VR1117936750.html?categoryid=20&cs=1.

Aaron Baker is an associate professor of film and media studies at Arizona State University and the author of *Contesting Identities: Sports in American Film.*

Books in the series
Contemporary Film Directors

The University of Illinois Press
is a founding member of the
Association of American University Presses.

_____

Designed by Paula Newcomb
Composed in 10/13 New Caledonia LT Std
with Helvetica Neue LT Std display
Composed by Barbara Evans
at the University of Illinois Press
Manufactured by Thomson-Shore, Inc.

University of Illinois Press
1325 South Oak Street
Champaign, IL 61820-6903
www.press.uillinois.edu